FREEZE & EASY

First published in the United Kingdom in 2013 by
PAVILION BOOKS
10 Southcombe Street
London W14 0RA

An imprint of Anova Books Company Ltd

Text © Sara Lewis
Design and layout © Anova Books 2013
Photography © Karen Thomas 2013

ISBN: 978-1-909108-02-8

A CIP record for this book is available from the British Library
10 9 8 7 6 5 4 3 2 1
Repro by Rival Colour Ltd, UK
Printed by 1010 Printing International Ltd, China

Senior commissioning editor: Becca Spry
Art director and cover: Georgina Hewitt
Design: Maru Studio
Photographer: Karen Thomas
Food styling: Sara Lewis
Food styling assistant: Andrew Lewis
Stylist: Wei Tang
Editor: Maggie Ramsay
Production: Laura Brodie

Paper swatches used throughout © PIE Books

Notes

- Medium eggs are used.
- Some dishes contain nuts or nut derivatives.
  It is advisable for those with known allergic
  reactions or who may be potentially vulnerable
  – pregnant and nursing mothers, invalids,
  the elderly, babies and children – to avoid
  these recipes.
- If using a fan-assisted oven, reduce the
  temperature by 10 or 20°C; see your
  manufacturer's handbook for details.
- Microwave timings have been tested in
  a 750 watt oven: if your machine is more
  powerful, reduce the timings slightly; increase
  timings for a lower wattage machine.

FREEZE & EASY

FABULOUS FOOD AND NEW IDEAS FOR MAKING THE MOST OF YOUR FREEZER

SARA LEWIS

PAVILION

CONTENTS

INTRODUCTION

How many of us really make the most of our freezer? Many of us buy things that are on special offer, freeze them and then forget about them, or make a dish for another day but neglect to label it before we freeze it. Most people store a loaf of bread, a pack of frozen peas and the all-important tub of ice-cream in the freezer. But it can do so much more. In this book you'll find recipes and tips to make your freezer really work for you, saving you time and money.

COOK TWO, FREEZE ONE
Having a big cook-up can really save time in the kitchen. You may need to allow an extra 15 minutes or so to chop veggies and prepare meat or fish, but the cooking time will be the same whether you are making one meal or two. Freeze in portion sizes that will be most useful to you: for four, two, or individual servings if your family eats at different times.

GIVE YOURSELF A BREAK
During the week, take out as many portions as you need and leave in the fridge to thaw overnight. Next day you've got a healthy 'ready meal' –

freeing you up to help to get on with your life.

BRILLIANT FOR BABY FOOD
Freeze smooth baby dinners in an ice-cube tray, then pop the frozen cubes into a plastic bag, and microwave when needed them. As your baby's appetite grows, simply thaw more ice-cubes at once. When he or she moves on to more roughly chopped food, pack mini-dinners in plastic containers. A word of warning: some microwaves heat unevenly, so stir the food once during reheating and once again before serving.

FAB FOR FADDY KIDS
Batch-cook and freeze your children's favourites and you'll always have a healthy supper at the ready.

GET AHEAD
If you have invited friends over, prepare some or all of the meal in advance and freeze it, so you can enjoy their company rather than being tied to the kitchen. The freezer really comes into its own at Christmas and on other special occasions, when there are so many things to prepare.

HOW TO USE YOUR FREEZER EFFICIENTLY

- A freezer needs to run at -18°C/0°F or lower. Some freezers have a digital indicator for easy checking; if yours doesn't, it's worth buying a small freezer thermometer.

- Don't site the freezer next to the cooker or a sunny window. Freestanding models need a little space at the back for air to circulate so that they work efficiently. Once a month – or, in real life, every three months – remove fluff and dust from the coils at the back to improve the efficiency of the freezer and reduce energy consumption.

- Wrap and label food before you freeze it.

- Never put warm or hot foods in the freezer. Cool cooked foods quickly by putting the container into a bowl of cold water with a large ice block.

- Sort through the freezer from time to time to check what's in there. You can freeze most cooked food for up to 2 months. Use up older items before newer ones that may be at the front or on top.

- Add no more than 10 per cent of the freezer capacity of previously unfrozen food at one time. If you are planning on adding lots of veggies from the garden or cooking for a party, think about doing it in a couple of batches. Set the freezer to fast-freeze so that it is extra-cold. Allow a little space between packages so that cold air can circulate freely. When the food is frozen, restack items close together.

- Most homegrown vegetables must be blanched before freezing (see page 68). Freeze as soon as possible after picking them.

- Freezers run more efficiently when full. If yours looks a bit empty, fill the gaps with a few loaves of bread, tubs of ice-cream or frozen veg.

- Open the door for as short a time as possible. It takes 30 minutes for the temperature to chill down again each time you open it. If there are young children in the house you might want to use a plastic freezer lock so the door doesn't get left open accidentally.

- Thaw the freezer every 6 months, or as soon as there is a build-up of ice.

SAVE MONEY

MAKE THE MOST OF SUPERMARKET OFFERS

Buy-one-get-one-free offers can be a genuine money-saver if you put the 'free one' straight into the freezer (assuming it is freezable). But check on the pack that the item hasn't been previously frozen.

BENEFIT FROM VEGETABLES AND FRUIT IN SEASON

A bumper crop in your garden or a visit to a pick-your-own farm can result in healthy and thrifty meals. Blanch vegetables and freeze in portions, make into soups and sauces, or use in casseroles and baked dishes. Even lettuce makes a delicious soup that can be frozen. Open-freeze berries (see page 112) before packing and labelling, or purée them with sugar and a squeeze of lemon juice to make a sauce for ice-creams and desserts, or to drizzle over yogurt for breakfast. Cook large batches of fruit with sugar and a little water or wine and flavour with finely grated lemon or orange zest, cinnamon or ginger to make a compote, pie filling or crumble base.

SAVE TIME AND MONEY WITH READY-FROZEN VEGETABLES

Frozen veg can be cheaper than their fresh counterparts, especially in winter, and are just as high in vitamins and minerals – in fact they often have a higher vitamin content because they haven't been hanging around in storage. Better to use some frozen veg than to buy fresh ones and not have time to use them so they go to waste.

FREEZE LEFTOVERS FROM A ROAST

Popping something into a freezer bag can save both money and time. But don't be tempted to freeze a pack of chicken breasts or minced (ground) beef that has been lurking in the fridge for a few days because you didn't get round to cooking it – by the time it's thawed it will be past its best.

- Freeze a leftover roast chicken carcass to make stock when you have time.
- If you have made too much gravy when cooking a roast, freeze the leftovers in a plastic bag; great for serving with sausages, or to use as the base for a savoury sauce.

MONEY-SAVING FREEZER TIPS

- That half-glass of wine left in the bottle can be frozen in an ice-cube tray and used to transform a gravy or sauce.

- Cut half a lemon into thin slices and freeze with water in an ice-cube tray for a stylish addition to drinks.

- Raw pancake or Yorkshire pudding batter freezes well.

- Blitz slightly stale bread in the food processor, then freeze the crumbs in a plastic bag. Use to coat fish cakes or sprinkle over gratins before grilling.

- Grate Cheddar, Parmesan or Gruyère cheese that has got a little dry around the edges, pack in a plastic bag and use straight from the freezer.

- Freeze leftover egg whites in a small plastic container and use to make meringues or a pavlova at a later date. Yolks or beaten egg can be frozen in an ice-cube tray. Don't freeze an egg in its shell or it will explode.

FREEZER TIMES

The low temperature of a freezer prevents potentially harmful bacteria from multiplying, but the flavour and appearance of food will gradually deteriorate, especially if it is not well packed. This can result in freezer burn, which is dehydration, resulting in greyish-white patches on the surface of food, especially meat and poultry. The patches are not harmful, just unsightly, and they can be cut off the food once thawed.

We've all come across packages at the back of the freezer that have been in there a little too long. Thaw the item slowly in the fridge and then inspect it carefully when fully thawed. If in doubt, throw it out.

COOKED OR PREPARED DISHES

1–2 months	cooked ham, pâté
	pancakes
	sandwiches
2–3 months	enriched bread dough, such as brioche
	raw biscuit (cookie) dough, uncooked pastry, crumble mix
	creamy mousses, homemade ice-cream or sorbet
3–4 months	tarts, quiches, pies
	cooked casseroles, gravy
	stock
	bread, breadcrumbs
	cakes
8–12 months	fruit compotes, cooked fruit fillings for pies and crumbles

UNCOOKED FOOD

1–2 months	bacon, sausages, hotdogs
	smoked fish
2–3 months	herring, mackerel, sardines, salmon and shellfish
3–4 months	raw minced (ground) beef, pork or lamb; raw meatballs and burgers
	unsalted butter, full-fat soft cheese or double (heavy) cream
	grated hard cheese
	chopped fresh herbs
	white fish
	duck (joints of whole)
6–8 months	full-fat hard cheese, such as Cheddar or Gruyère
	salted butter
	jointed chicken and whole game birds
	beef, lamb or pork steaks, chops or diced meat
	green vegetables, blanched
	tomatoes (open-freeze, then pack)
	whole Seville oranges
	halved stoned fruits, such as peaches and plums
12 months	whole chicken
	leg of lamb, joint of beef or pork
	summer berries (open-freeze, then pack, purée or cook as a compote)
	raw egg whites or yolks (add a little salt or sugar to yolks), frozen separately or as beaten eggs

THAWING AND REHEATING

Many of the recipes in this book can be reheated straight from the freezer. Some can be thawed in the microwave, others overnight in the fridge.

Thawing time depends on the size and type of container and the depth of the frozen food. Meat, poultry and dairy foods are best thawed in the fridge. However, for larger quantities this can take up to 2 days. To speed up the process, you can immerse food in a well-sealed plastic bag in cold water and change the water frequently. Never thaw poultry, meat or fish by immersing in hot water.

Bacteria are not destroyed through freezing. Once a dish is taken out of the freezer to thaw, any bacteria present can multiply. Food should be brought up to 70°C/158°F for 2 minutes; test it with a meat thermometer, or check that sauces are bubbling all over the surface. This is especially important when reheating baby food (obviously you should allow this to cool before serving it). Stir food at least once during reheating so that it reheats evenly; it must be hot throughout.

Do not reheat cooked food more than once. Once food has thawed, do not refreeze it.

HELP – THE FREEZER HAS BEEN TURNED OFF!
In the case of a power cut, do not open the freezer door – and warn the rest of the family not to open it. A packed freezer should stay cold for up to 12 hours, or best-case scenario up to 36 hours.

When the power comes back on, or if the freezer has been off for longer than 12 hours, take everything out and sort through it. Set the freezer to fast-freeze. Anything that is still frozen hard can go back into the freezer, after you have wiped off any moisture. Frozen vegetables, bread and puff pastry can be put back if partly frozen, but aim to use them up within a few weeks. Use partly thawed frozen fruit to make jam, adding an extra 10 per cent of fruit to your recipe. Cooked food or shellfish that has defrosted cannot go back in the freezer. Anything else that is raw and has begun to thaw will need to be thawed fully, cooked, cooled and refrozen. Ice-cream that is partly thawed must be discarded.

STORAGE TIPS

Choose freezer containers that suit your lifestyle: single servings if you live on your own or your family often eats at different times; four- or six-serving containers for meals you plan to share.

When reusing plastic containers such as ice-cream tubs, check that the lids fit well. For family suppers that can be cooked straight from the freezer, you can buy 23cm/9in square foil containers with lids, or smaller versions for individual servings. A selection of freezer-to-microwave dishes can be a good investment. Identical containers use space efficiently.

Ovenproof china dishes can be used in the freezer, but avoid glass, as it may shatter. However, rather than 'losing' a dish in the freezer you can line it with foil before adding the food; freeze until solid, then lift out and wrap well. To thaw and serve, peel away the foil and replace the food in the dish.

'Boil in the bags' are useful for rice or vegetables as they can go straight from the freezer to a pan of boiling water. Plastic bags with a gusset are more stable when filling with soup. Store grated cheese, breadcrumbs or crumble topping in ziplock bags that you can dip into and reseal.

Freeze soups and sauces in stackable brick shapes to make best use of freezer space. Put a plastic bag into a loaf tin, then fill and freeze; remove the tin once the food is frozen. If using metal ties, remove them before thawing the food in the microwave.

Leave a 2cm/¾in space when filling dishes, especially for liquids such as soup, as water expands during freezing.

Wrap meat and poultry closely with clingfilm (plastic wrap) or foil so that it won't dry out and get freezer burn.

Use freezerproof labels and label foods clearly with their recipe title, the date you froze them and the 'use-by' date. You always think you will remember what's in the box – but a few months later it can be hard to tell the difference between a frozen casserole and a fruit compote. Coloured labels or coloured pens can help you locate different foods: perhaps red labels for meat, blue for fish and so on.

MEAT

MEAT

Dinner ready and waiting sounds almost too good to be true, especially after a manic day at work or ferrying kids here and there. How about spicy slow-cooked beef with sweet potatoes or sausage and lentil stew with garlic and herb bread that can be reheated from frozen in the microwave? If you can plan a day ahead and leave a meal to thaw in the fridge overnight, why not look forward to beef and mustard hotpot, slow-cooked belly pork with richly flavoured beans, or lamb rogan josh? For a family get-together you can pull a complete roast dinner out of the freezer as if by magic: roast leg of lamb, a summer vegetable medley of peas, broad beans (fava beans) and green beans, and goose-fat-roasted potatoes.

Before freezing raw meat, it makes sense to repackage the meat into usable portions: a large pack of chicken thighs will be impossible to separate into 4 or 8 pieces once frozen as a block.

The freezer really comes into its own in preparation for large gatherings such as Christmas or Thanksgiving. Stuffing, bacon rolls, sauces and gravy can all be made in advance to save you time on the day (see pages 40–43).

When reheating food, make sure meat is piping hot right through to the centre. To test, put the blade of a small, sharp knife into the meat, leave for 10 seconds, then take out and briefly touch the blade: it should be hot. Pork and chicken should show no signs of pink juices. If you are unsure, cook the dish for a little longer and then retest. Stir sauced dishes to even out the heat.

ROAST LAMB
READY AND WAITING

Family and friends love to share a traditional roast dinner, and here's a way to prepare everything – meat, potatoes and vegetables – so that it is ready to go straight into the oven from the freezer. What could be easier?

SERVES 6–8

PREP: 30 MINUTES

COOK FROM FROZEN: 2½–3 HOURS

Rosemary roast potatoes

1.5kg/3lb 5oz BAKING POTATOES, CUT INTO CHUNKS

115g/4oz/½ CUP GOOSE FAT

3 SPRIGS OF FRESH ROSEMARY

6 GARLIC CLOVES, FINELY CHOPPED

SEA SALT AND FRESHLY GROUND BLACK PEPPER

Summer vegetable medley

500g/1lb 2oz BROAD BEANS (FAVA BEANS) IN
    PODS, SHELLED

200g/7oz GREEN BEANS, TOPS TRIMMED

500g/1lb 2oz PEAS IN PODS, SHELLED

2 SMALL LEEKS, CUT INTO 1cm/½in SLICES

40g/1½oz/3 TBSP BUTTER

FINELY GRATED ZEST OF 1 UNWAXED LEMON

SMALL HANDFUL OF FRESH PARSLEY, ROUGHLY CHOPPED

4 TSP CAPERS, DRAINED AND CHOPPED (OPTIONAL)

Roast lamb

1.8kg/4lb FROZEN PART-BONED LEG OF LAMB

2 TBSP OLIVE OIL

3 GARLIC CLOVES, FINELY CHOPPED

½ TSP SMOKED HOT PAPRIKA

1 TSP BLACK PEPPERCORNS, ROUGHLY CRUSHED

LEAVES FROM 3 SPRIGS OF ROSEMARY, ROUGHLY CHOPPED

To serve

450ml/16fl oz/2 CUPS LAMB STOCK

4 TBSP DRY SHERRY OR PORT

1 TBSP REDCURRANT JELLY

---

1. Put the potatoes in a saucepan of lightly salted boiling water, bring back to the boil and cook for about 10 minutes, until almost tender. Drain in a colander, shaking it to roughen the edges. Melt the goose fat in the drained saucepan and use a little to brush a large foil roasting dish. Add the potatoes, rosemary, garlic, salt and pepper to the roasting dish, then pour the remaining goose fat over. Leave to cool, then cover with the lid. Freeze.

2. For the vegetables, put the broad beans and green beans in a large saucepan of boiling water and cook for 2 minutes. Add the peas and leeks and cook for another minute. Drain well, then transfer to a large freezer bag. Add the butter, lemon zest, parsley and capers, if using, plus a little salt and pepper. Leave to cool completely, then seal the bag, pressing out as much air as possible. Freeze.

3. Put the frozen lamb on a large piece of foil. Mix the oil, garlic and paprika with salt and the crushed peppercorns, then brush over the lamb and sprinkle with the chopped rosemary. Wrap the foil around the lamb to enclose tightly. Freeze.

Recipe continues...

To freeze
At the end of step 3, label all containers and freeze for up to 2 months.

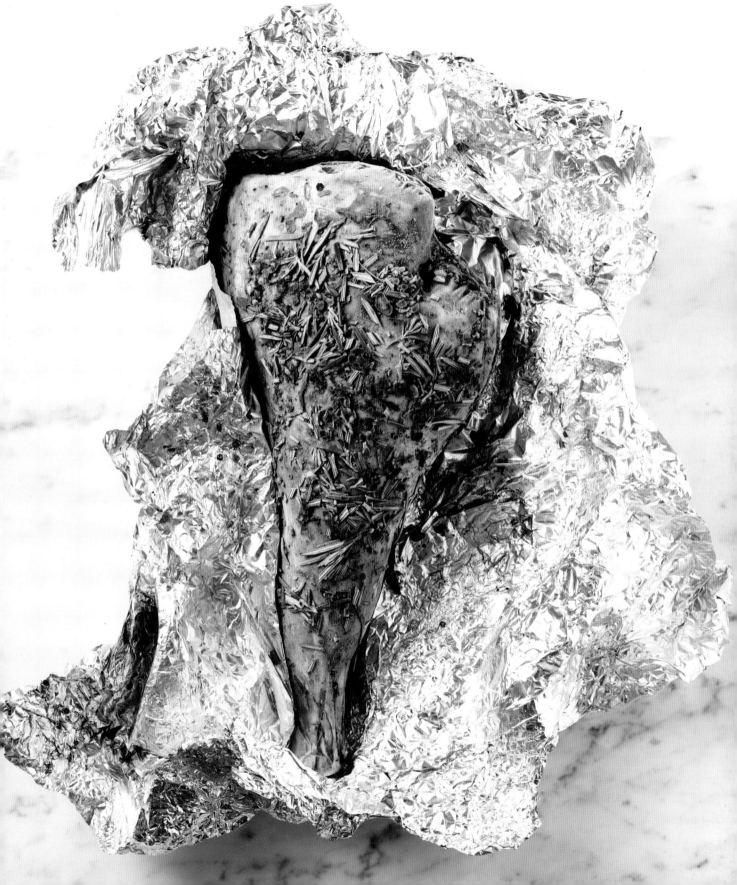

Preheat the oven to 140°C/275°C/Gas Mark 1. Take the lamb, potatoes and green veg out of the freezer. Unwrap the lamb, place in a roasting pan and loosely cover with the same foil. Roast on the middle shelf of the oven for 1 hour. Remove the foil, baste with pan juices and increase the oven to 190°C/375°F/Gas Mark 5. Remove the lid from the frozen potatoes and put them on the shelf below the lamb. Roast for 1½ hours for pink lamb or 1 hour 50 minutes for well done lamb, basting once or twice and turning the potatoes once or twice until golden brown. After 45 minutes, tip the potatoes out into a large roasting tin for the rest of the cooking.

Transfer the lamb to a serving plate, cover with the foil and leave to rest for 10 minutes. Tip the partly thawed vegetables into a saucepan, cover and cook gently for 5–8 minutes, stirring from time to time, until hot.

Meanwhile, pour off most of the fat from the roasting pan to leave just 3 tbsp, then add the stock, sherry and redcurrant jelly and bring to the boil, scraping up the meat juices from the bottom of the pan. Boil for 2 minutes, then strain into a serving jug.

Carve the lamb and serve with the roast potatoes, vegetables and gravy.

LAMB
ROGAN JOSH

SERVES 4

PREP: 15 MINUTES

COOK: 2¼ HOURS

REHEAT FROM FROZEN: THAW OVERNIGHT,
    REHEAT 25–30 MINUTES IN A SAUCEPAN

1 TBSP SUNFLOWER OIL

4 X 300–350g/10–12oz LAMB SHANKS

2 ONIONS, HALVED AND SLICED

4 GARLIC CLOVES, FINELY CHOPPED

4cm/1½in PIECE FRESH GINGER, PEELED AND
    FINELY CHOPPED

1 CINNAMON STICK, HALVED

8 GREEN CARDAMOM PODS, CRUSHED

4 TBSP MEDIUM-HOT CURRY PASTE

2 TBSP PLAIN (ALL-PURPOSE) FLOUR

2 TBSP TOMATO PUREE (TOMATO PASTE)

2 TSP CASTER (SUPERFINE) SUGAR

500g/1lb 2oz TOMATOES (PEELED IF YOU LIKE),
    ROUGHLY CHOPPED

600ml/1 PINT/2½ CUPS LAMB OR CHICKEN STOCK

SALT AND FRESHLY GROUND BLACK PEPPER

PILAU RICE, TO SERVE (SEE PAGE 22)

FRESH CORIANDER (CILANTRO), TO GARNISH (OPTIONAL)

Lamb shanks are slow-cooked so that the meat is meltingly tender, bathed in a tomato-based curry with a well-rounded flavour. Pilau rice can be prepared in advance and frozen for a quick accompaniment to any curry.

1. Preheat the oven to 180°C/350°F/Gas Mark 4. Heat the oil in a frying pan, add the lamb shanks and cook for 10 minutes, turning until browned all over. Transfer the lamb shanks to an ovenproof casserole dish in which they fit snugly.

2. Add the onions to the frying pan and cook for 5 minutes until just beginning to turn golden. Stir in the garlic, ginger, cinnamon and cardamom. Mix in the curry paste and cook for 1 minute.

3. Mix in the flour, tomato purée and sugar, then add the tomatoes and stock. Season well with salt and pepper, bring to the boil, then pour over the lamb. Cover the dish and cook in the oven for 2 hours, until tender.

4. Serve hot, with the pilau rice, garnished with torn coriander leaves if liked.

Recipe continues...

To serve from frozen
Thaw completely overnight in the fridge. Transfer to a saucepan, bring to the boil, cover and cook over a medium heat for 25–30 minutes until the lamb is piping hot right through.

To freeze
At the end of step 3, leave to cool completely. Pack in a large plastic bag or container, seal and label. Freeze for up to 2 months.

LAMB
...CONTINUED

ALSO TRY THIS MOROCCAN-STYLE LAMB SHANKS

Brown 4 lamb shanks in 1 tbsp olive oil and transfer to a casserole dish. Fry 2 sliced onions in sunflower oil. Stir in 4 finely chopped garlic cloves and 1 tbsp roughly crushed coriander seeds and fry for 1 minute. Mix in 1 finely chopped unwaxed lemon (including flesh and skin), 2 tbsp plain (all-purpose) flour, 3 sprigs of rosemary, 1 tbsp tomato purée (tomato paste), 500g/1lb 2oz chopped tomatoes and 600ml/1 pint/2½ cups lamb stock. Season, pour over the lamb and cook as on page 21, step 3. Serve with cooked couscous, flavoured with chopped fresh herbs and a little olive oil.

PILAU RICE

Rinse 250g/9oz/generous 1¼ cups basmati rice in cold water, then soak for 15 minutes. Heat 25g/1oz/2 tbsp butter and 1 tbsp sunflower oil in a saucepan, add 1 finely chopped onion and cook gently for 5 minutes until softened. Add 6 crushed cardamom pods, 1 halved cinnamon stick, 4 cloves, ¼ tsp turmeric and 2 bay leaves and cook for 1 minute. Drain the rice and stir into the spices. Pour in 500ml/17fl oz/2¼ cups boiling water, add salt and pepper, cover and simmer for 10 minutes. Take off the heat and leave to stand for 8–10 minutes. Serve immediately or freeze.

To serve the pilau rice from frozen
Microwave on full power, in the bag minus the metal tie, for 3 minutes. Tip into a shallow bowl, break up with a fork, cover and cook for 6-8 minutes, until hot.

To freeze the pilau rice
Leave to cool. Pack into a plastic bag and seal and label. Freeze for up to 2 months.

SLOW-COOKED BELLY PORK
WITH CHORIZO AND BEANS

Belly pork is an inexpensive cut that cooks to melting tenderness. This dish can be frozen in single portions for a warming dinner.

SERVES 4	
PREP: 25 MINUTES	
COOK: 2½ HOURS	
REHEAT FROM FROZEN: THAW OVERNIGHT, REHEAT 40–45 MINUTES	

1–1.1kg/2¼–2½lb PIECE BELLY PORK, CUT INTO 4 SQUARES

COARSE SEA SALT

1 TSP FENNEL SEEDS, ROUGHLY CRUSHED

400g CAN CANNELLINI BEANS, RINSED AND DRAINED

400g CAN CHOPPED TOMATOES

115g/4oz CHORIZO SAUSAGE, SLICED OR DICED

3 GARLIC CLOVES, FINELY CHOPPED

3 SPRIGS OF FRESH THYME

1 LARGE RED ONION, ROUGHLY CHOPPED

6 MIXED RED, YELLOW AND ORANGE PEPPERS, QUARTERED AND DESEEDED

FRESHLY GROUND BLACK PEPPER

1. Preheat the oven to 220°C/425°F/Gas Mark 7. Score the skin of the pork using a very sharp knife, then rub it with the salt and fennel seeds. Put into a large roasting pan and cook for 30 minutes.

2. Lift the pork out of the roasting pan and set aside. Reduce the oven temperature to 150°C/300°F/Gas Mark 2. Put the beans, tomatoes, chorizo, garlic and thyme in the roasting pan and mix together, then add the onion and peppers and sprinkle with black pepper. Arrange the pork on top, skin side up. Return to the oven and cook for 2 hours until the pork is deep golden, cooked through and very tender.

3. If the pork skin is not crisp, put the roasting pan under a preheated grill, shielding the pepper mixture with foil, and grill for 5–10 minutes until the skin is crisp.

4. To serve, transfer the pepper mixture to 4 large shallow bowls, discarding the thyme stems. Arrange the pork on top, carved into slices if preferred.

To serve from frozen
Thaw completely overnight in the fridge. Preheat the oven to 180°C/350°C/Gas Mark 4. Remove the lids and heat for 40-45 minutes until the pork is piping hot right through.

To freeze
At the end of step 3, leave to cool completely. Divide the pepper mixture and pork among 4 foil containers, add the lids, seal and label. Freeze for up to 2 months.

CHIPOTLE-SPICED PORK TORTILLAS

This spicy pork stew is cooked with tomatoes and red kidney beans in a sauce that includes chipotle chillies and coffee for a deep mellow heat with just a hint of smokiness. Serve with warmed tortillas, sour cream and grated cheese.

SERVES 4

PREP: 20 MINUTES

COOK: 1¼–1½ HOURS

REHEAT FROM FROZEN: 10 MINUTES IN THE MICROWAVE OR 25 MINUTES IN A SAUCEPAN

1–2 LARGE DRIED CHIPOTLE CHILLIES
125ml/4fl oz/½ CUP HOT STRONG BLACK COFFEE OR 2 TSP INSTANT COFFEE IN 125ml/4fl oz/½ CUP BOILING WATER
1 TBSP OLIVE OIL
600g/1lb 5oz LEAN SHOULDER OF PORK, CUBED
2 RED ONIONS, ROUGHLY CHOPPED
2 GARLIC CLOVES, FINELY CHOPPED
1 RED PEPPER, DESEEDED AND DICED
1 MILD GREEN CHILLI, DESEEDED IF LIKED, CHOPPED
1 TSP ALLSPICE BERRIES, ROUGHLY CRUSHED
1 TSP GROUND CINNAMON
1 TSP DRIED OREGANO
400g CAN CHOPPED TOMATOES
400g CAN RED KIDNEY BEANS, RINSED AND DRAINED
300ml/10fl oz/1¼ CUPS CHICKEN STOCK
SALT AND FRESHLY GROUND BLACK PEPPER

To serve

SOFT FLOUR TORTILLAS
SOUR CREAM OR CRÈME FRAÎCHE
GRATED MONTEREY JACK OR CHEDDAR CHEESE, GRATED

1. Soak the dried chipotle chillies in the hot coffee for 5 minutes.

2. Heat the oil in a large saucepan over a medium heat. Add the pork a few pieces at a time until it is all in the pan, stirring until lightly browned. Add the onions and cook for 5 minutes, stirring from time to time until they begin to brown.

3. Stir in the garlic, red pepper and green chilli and cook for 2 minutes. Mix in all the remaining ingredients, including the soaked chillies and coffee. Bring to the boil, stirring, then cover and simmer gently for 1¼– 1½ hours, stirring from time to time, until the pork is tender.

4. To serve, warm the tortillas and spoon on the pork mixture. Serve with a spoonful of sour cream and a sprinkling of grated cheese.

To freeze
At the end of step 3, leave to cool completely. Pack into 4 individual containers, cover, seal and label. Freeze for up to 2 months.

To serve from frozen
Microwave one portion at a time for 10 minutes, stir well and leave to stand for 5 minutes before serving. Or cook one portion at a time in a covered saucepan on a low heat for 25 minutes, stirring frequently, and gradually increasing the heat until piping hot.

BEEF AND MUSTARD
HOTPOT

Make up a large casserole to serve 8, then split and serve two ways: as a hotpot, topped with golden sliced potatoes, or as a casserole with light herb dumplings. You could also serve the casserole as it is, with mashed potatoes, or cover it with puff pastry and bake it as a pie.

SERVES 4, TWICE

PREP: 30 MINUTES

COOK: 2¼ HOURS

REHEAT FROM FROZEN: THAW 12–18 HOURS, REHEAT
    1 HOUR–1 HOUR 10 MINUTES FOR THE HOTPOT,
    30–35 MINUTES FOR CASSEROLE WITH DUMPLINGS

2 TBSP SUNFLOWER OIL

1.25kg/2lb 12oz LEAN BRAISING BEEF, CUBED

2 ONIONS, FINELY CHOPPED

4 TBSP PLAIN (ALL-PURPOSE) FLOUR

1 LITRE/1¾ PINTS/4 CUPS BEEF STOCK

2 TBSP WHOLEGRAIN MUSTARD

2 TBSP LIGHT BROWN SUGAR

3 BAY LEAVES

SALT AND FRESHLY GROUND BLACK PEPPER

500g/1lb 2oz CHANTENAY BABY CARROTS,
    SCRUBBED, LEFT WHOLE

350g/12oz SWEDE (RUTABAGA),
    CUT INTO CUBES THE SAME SIZE AS THE BEEF

2 LEEKS, WHITE PART THICKLY SLICED,
    GREEN PART THINLY SLICED

1. Preheat the oven to 160°C/325°F/Gas Mark 3. Heat 1 tbsp of the oil in a large frying pan, add the beef, a few pieces at a time, and cook, turning, until browned all over. Using a slotted spoon, transfer to a large casserole dish. Cook all the beef in the same way, adding more oil as needed. Cook the onions in the same pan for 5 minutes until softened and just beginning to brown.

2. Sprinkle the flour over the onions, stir, then gradually stir in the stock and bring to the boil. Stir in the mustard, sugar, bay leaves and plenty of salt and pepper. Pour over the beef, cover and cook in the oven for 1¼ hours.

3. Stir the carrots, swede and white leek slices into the casserole and return to the oven for 45 minutes, until tender.

Recipe continues…

To freeze the hotpot

At the end of step 4 (see page 27), spoon half the casserole into a foil-lined ovenproof dish. Arrange the boiled sliced potatoes over the beef and brush with the melted butter and mustard mixture. Cover with foil, seal and label, then leave to cool completely. Freeze until firm. Take the frozen casserole out of the dish, check it is completely wrapped, then return to the freezer for up to 3 months. Spoon the other half of the casserole into a plastic bag, seal and label.

To serve from frozen

Peel away the foil and return the hotpot to the dish. Cover the top with foil and thaw in the fridge for 12–18 hours, or until completely thawed. Preheat the oven to 190°C/375°F/Gas Mark 5. Remove the foil and place the hotpot in the oven for 1 hour–1 hour 10 minutes, until piping hot. Check after 30 minutes and loosely cover with foil if the potatoes are browning too quickly.

HOTPOT
...CONTINUED

4. Blanch the green leek slices in boiling water for 2 minutes until just softened. Drain and stir into the casserole.

5. Divide the casserole in half and finish with either the hotpot topping or dumplings – or freeze 'topless'.

HOTPOT TOPPING

Increase the oven to 190°C/375°F/ Gas Mark 5. Cook 680g/1½lb thinly sliced, peeled potatoes in boiling water for 4–5 minutes until just tender, then drain. Arrange overlapping over half the beef, in a casserole dish. Melt 40g/1½oz/3 tbsp butter and mix with 2 tsp wholegrain mustard, then brush over the potatoes. Place in the oven for 45–50 minutes, until the potatoes are golden brown and crisp.

DUMPLINGS

Mix 140g/5oz/generous 1 cup self-raising flour with 85g/3oz shredded suet. Add a handful of finely chopped fresh parsley or chives and salt and pepper. Gradually stir in 5–6 tbsp cold water and mix to form a soft dough. Cut into 8, then shape into balls, using floured hands. To serve now: reheat half the casserole in a saucepan until piping hot, add the dumplings, cover and simmer for about 15 minutes until the dumplings are light and fluffy. Serve in shallow bowls.

To freeze the dumplings
Open-freeze the dumplings on a baking sheet until firm, then pack into a plastic bag, seal and label. Freeze for up to 2 months.

To serve from frozen
Thaw half the beef casserole in the fridge for 12–18 hours. Reheat in a large saucepan for 10 minutes, until boiling. Arrange the frozen dumplings in a ring on top, cover and simmer gently for 20–25 minutes, until the dumplings are light, fluffy and piping hot.

BEEF AND SWEET POTATO ADOBO

SERVES 8

PREP: 25 MINUTES

COOK: 2¼ HOURS

REHEAT FROM FROZEN: 10 MINUTES IN THE MICROWAVE OR
25 MINUTES IN A SAUCEPAN

1.25kg/2lb 12oz LEAN BRAISING BEEF, CUBED
3 TBSP PLAIN (ALL-PURPOSE) FLOUR
SALT AND FRESHLY GROUND BLACK PEPPER
3 TBSP SUNFLOWER OIL
2 ONIONS, FINELY CHOPPED
2–3 GARLIC CLOVES, FINELY CHOPPED
1 TSP DRIED CRUSHED RED CHILLIES
6 TBSP SOY SAUCE
6 TBSP MALT VINEGAR
2 TBSP LIGHT BROWN SUGAR
2 BAY LEAVES
750ml/1¼ PINTS/3 CUPS BEEF STOCK
900g/2lb SWEET POTATOES,
   CUT INTO CUBES THE SAME SIZE AS THE BEEF
CHINESE EGG NOODLES, COOKED, TO SERVE
HANDFUL OF FRESH CORIANDER (CILANTRO), TO SERVE

Adobo is a Filipino casserole flavoured with soy sauce, chillies and vinegar; this version is made with beef. Making a big casserole and freezing it in individual portions is a great way to cope with the demands of a busy family.

1. Preheat the oven to 160°C/325°F/Gas Mark 3. Put the beef in a large plastic bag with the flour and plenty of salt and pepper. Shake until the beef is evenly coated.

2. Heat 1 tbsp of the oil in a frying pan, add the onions and cook for 5 minutes, stirring from time to time, until just beginning to brown. Using a slotted spoon, transfer to a large casserole dish.

3. Add 1 tbsp oil to the pan and heat, then add the beef, a few pieces at a time and cook, turning, until browned all over. Transfer to the casserole dish and continue browning the beef in batches, adding more oil as needed.

4. Add the garlic and chillies to the remaining pan juices, followed by the soy sauce, vinegar, sugar and bay. Pour in the stock and bring to the boil, stirring, then pour over the beef and onions. Cover and cook in the oven for 1¼ hours.

5. Stir in the sweet potatoes and return to the oven for 45 minutes, until the potatoes and beef are tender.

6. To serve, spoon some cooked Chinese egg noodles into bowls, spoon in some of the hot adobo and garnish with torn coriander. Serve with stir-fried pak choi.

To serve from frozen

Thaw one portion at a time in the microwave for 10 minutes on full power, stirring twice, until piping hot. Or reheat in a covered saucepan for 25 minutes, over a low heat to begin with, stirring and increasing the heat as the dish thaws, until piping hot.

For 4 portions, defrost in the fridge overnight then reheat for 20–25 minutes in a covered saucepan.

To freeze
At the end of step 5, leave the adobo to cool. Pack 8 individual portions into plastic bags, seal and label. Freeze for up to 3 months.

STIR-FRIED PAK CHOI

Heat 1 tbsp sesame oil in a wok, add 2 heads thickly sliced pak choi (bok choy), 2cm/¾in fresh ginger, finely chopped, and a little dried crushed red chilli. Stir-fry for 2 minutes and serve immediately.

VENISON SAUSAGE AND LENTIL STEW
WITH HERBY GARLIC CROUTES

Quick to cook, this tasty sausage supper is made with venison sausages, but you could use Toulouse sausages, merguez or others instead.

SERVES 4
PREP: 20 MINUTES
COOK: 30 MINUTES
REHEAT FROM FROZEN: 10 MINUTES IN THE MICROWAVE
    OR 20–25 MINUTES IN A SAUCEPAN

25g/1oz/¾ CUP DRIED PORCINI MUSHROOMS
375ml/13fl oz/1½ CUPS BOILING WATER
175g/6oz/SCANT 1 CUP PUY LENTILS, RINSED
1 TBSP OLIVE OIL
1 ONION, FINELY CHOPPED
2 GARLIC CLOVES, FINELY CHOPPED
400g/14oz POTATOES, CUBED
½ TSP SMOKED HOT PAPRIKA
400g/14oz CAN CHOPPED TOMATOES
175ml/6 fl oz/¾ CUP RED WINE OR STOCK
1 TBSP REDCURRANT JELLY
2 LARGE SPRIGS OF FRESH THYME
SALT AND FRESHLY GROUND BLACK PEPPER
8 LARGE VENISON SAUSAGES

Croutes

55g/2oz/4 TBSP BUTTER, AT ROOM TEMPERATURE
2 GARLIC CLOVES, FINELY CHOPPED
LEAVES FROM 2 SPRIGS OF FRESH THYME, CHOPPED
SMALL HANDFUL OF FRESH PARSLEY, CHOPPED
8 SLICES OF FRENCH BREAD OR CIABATTA

1. Soak the dried mushrooms in the measured boiling water for 15 minutes. Put the lentils in a saucepan, cover with boiling water, bring to the boil and simmer for 20 minutes, until almost tender.

2. Meanwhile, heat the oil in a saucepan, add the onion and cook for 5 minutes, stirring from time to time, until just beginning to brown. Add the garlic, potatoes and paprika and cook for 1 minute, then stir in the tomatoes, wine or stock, redcurrant jelly and thyme. Mix well and season with salt and pepper. Cover and simmer for 10 minutes. Preheat the grill to medium–high.

3. Grill the sausages for 10 minutes, turning, until evenly browned. Cut into thick slices.

4. Drain the lentils, then add to the tomato mixture with the soaked mushrooms and their liquid and the sliced sausages. Cover and cook for 10 minutes.

5. To make the croutes, beat the butter with the garlic, herbs and a little black pepper. Lightly toast the bread on both sides, then spread liberally with the herb butter.

6. To serve, spoon the stew into shallow bowls. Grill the croutes until golden and serve on top of the stew.

To freeze

Cool the stew at the end of step 4, then pack into individual plastic dishes or bags. Seal, label and freeze for up to 3 months. Open-freeze the croutes on a baking sheet until firm, then pack into a plastic box, seal, label and freeze.

To serve from frozen

Microwave one portion at a time on full power for 5 minutes, tip into a serving dish, stir and cook for 5 minutes until piping hot. Or reheat in a covered saucepan for 20–25 minutes until piping hot, breaking up and stirring from time to time. Grill the croutes under a low heat for 5 minutes, then serve on top of the lentils.

PHEASANT PIE

When you invite friends for supper you can spend time chatting rather than chopping if you make good use of your freezer and prepare the meal the week before. If you are not a fan of pheasant, use 4 chicken thighs and 4 chicken drumsticks instead.

SERVES 4

PREP: 45 MINUTES

COOK: 1 HOUR 25 MINUTES

COOK FROM FROZEN: THAW OVERNIGHT,
    COOK 40–45 MINUTES

2 PREPARED PHEASANT
25g/1oz/2 TBSP BUTTER
2 TBSP OLIVE OIL
1 ONION, FINELY CHOPPED
100g/3½oz SMOKED BACK BACON OR PANCETTA, DICED
2 TBSP PLAIN (ALL-PURPOSE) FLOUR,
    PLUS EXTRA FOR DUSTING
250ml/8fl oz/1 CUP RED WINE
250ml/8fl oz/1 CUP CHICKEN STOCK
2 TBSP CRANBERRY SAUCE
1 TSP ALLSPICE BERRIES, ROUGHLY CRUSHED
1 BOUQUET GARNI
SEA SALT AND FRESHLY GROUND BLACK PEPPER
250g/9oz SHALLOTS, PEELED
140g/5oz BUTTON MUSHROOMS
350g/12oz CHILLED PUFF PASTRY
BEATEN EGG, TO GLAZE

1. Preheat the oven to 160°C/325°F/Gas Mark 3. Rinse the pheasant inside and out, drain and pat dry.

2. Heat the butter and 1 tbsp of the oil in a frying pan over a medium heat and brown the pheasant all over. Transfer to a casserole dish. Add the onion and bacon or pancetta to the pan and cook for 5 minutes, stirring. Stir in the flour, then add the wine, stock, cranberry sauce, allspice and bouquet garni. Season well and pour into the casserole dish. Cover and cook in the oven for 1¼ hours.

3. Leave to cool. Lift the pheasant out of the sauce. Discard the skin and take the meat off the bones. Cut the meat into bite-size pieces and place in a 1.2-litre/2-pint pie dish.

4. Cook the shallots in the frying pan in 1 tbsp oil over a medium heat for 5 minutes. Add the mushrooms and cook until lightly browned. Add to the pie dish, followed by the sauce, discarding the bouquet garni.

5. Roll out the pastry on a lightly floured surface until a little larger than the top of the pie dish. Cut a 1cm/½in strip from the edge. Brush the rim of the dish with water, stick the pastry strip on the rim and brush with water. Lift the remaining pastry over the rolling pin and unroll over the pie. Press the pastry lid to the rim, then trim the edge. Knock up and flute the edge with a small knife. Cut leaf shapes from the pastry trimmings and stick to the pie with a little water.

6. To serve, brush with beaten egg and sprinkle with sea salt and coarsley crushed pepper, bake at 200°C/400°F/Gas Mark 6 for 30–35 minutes.

To serve from frozen

Thaw completely overnight in the fridge or for a minimum of 12 hours. Preheat the oven to 200°C/400°F/Gas Mark 6. Remove the clingfilm, brush the pastry with beaten egg, sprinkle with sea salt and pepper and bake for 40-45 minutes until the pastry is golden brown and the filling is bubbling and piping hot.

To freeze

At the end of step 5, open-freeze the pie with uncooked pie crust until firm. Wrap in clingfilm, seal and label. Freeze for up to 2 months.

GOAN CHICKEN AND SPINACH CURRY

A mellow blend of coconut milk with tamarind, green chillies and cumin finished with fresh spinach, coriander and mint leaves. The sauce is vibrant green. Serve with naan bread (see page 103) and spoons to scoop up all the delicious sauce.

SERVES 4

PREP: 20 MINUTES

COOK: 35 MINUTES

REHEAT FROM FROZEN: THAW OVERNIGHT, REHEAT 10 MINUTES IN A SAUCEPAN

1 TBSP SUNFLOWER OIL

350g/12oz POTATOES, CUT INTO 2cm/¾in CUBES

400ml CAN FULL-FAT COCONUT MILK

250ml/8fl oz/1 CUP CHICKEN STOCK

SALT AND FRESHLY GROUND BLACK PEPPER

600g/1lb 5oz (4 MEDIUM) SKINLESS, BONELESS CHICKEN BREASTS, SLICED

250g/9oz YOUNG SPINACH, WASHED, DRAINED

LARGE HANDFUL OF FRESH CORIANDER (CILANTRO)

SMALL HANDFUL OF FRESH MINT

Curry paste

2 GREEN 'FINGER' CHILLIES, THICKLY SLICED, INCLUDING SEEDS FOR EXTRA HEAT IF LIKED

2 GARLIC CLOVES, PEELED

1 ONION, QUARTERED

1 TSP CUMIN SEEDS

1 TSP GROUND CORIANDER

2 TSP TAMARIND PULP

2 TSP PALM SUGAR OR CASTER (SUPERFINE) SUGAR

To serve

TOASTED FLAKED ALMONDS OR EXTRA HERBS, TO GARNISH

NAAN BREADS, WARMED, TO SERVE

1. Put all the curry paste ingredients in a food processor or blender and blitz until finely chopped.

2. Heat the oil in a saucepan, add the curry paste and cook for 2 minutes, stirring. Add the potatoes, stir to coat in the paste and cook for 2–3 minutes, stirring, until beginning to brown.

3. Pour in the coconut milk and 125ml/4fl oz/½ cup stock, season well with salt and pepper, bring to the boil, cover and simmer for 10 minutes. Stir the chicken into the sauce, cover and cook for 10–15 minutes, until the chicken and potatoes are cooked through.

4. Finely chop the spinach and herbs, stir into the sauce, bring to the boil and cook for 2 minutes. Add the remaining stock if needed, taste and adjust the seasoning.

5. To serve, simmer for another 2–3 minutes, then serve in shallow bowls. Garnish with toasted flaked almonds or extra herbs and serve with warmed naan breads

To serve from frozen

Thaw overnight in the fridge. Transfer to a saucepan, bring to the boil and cook for 10 minutes, stirring, until piping hot. Serve as above.

To freeze

At the end of step 4, leave to cool completely. Pack into 4 containers, seal and label. Freeze for up to 3 months.

CHICKEN AND
WILD MUSHROOM
LASAGNE

Chicken thighs are given a gourmet makeover in this pasta dish, topped with creamy smooth mascarpone and Parmesan and baked for a golden bubbling crust. The choice of mushrooms could include chestnut, oyster, shiitake or button.

SERVES 4–6

PREP: 30 MINUTES

COOK: 55 MINUTES

COOK FROM FROZEN: THAW OVERNIGHT,
    COOK 50–60 MINUTES

750g/1lb 10oz CHICKEN THIGHS ON THE BONE

3 SPRIGS OF FRESH THYME

175ml/6fl oz/¾ CUP DRY WHITE WINE

750ml/1¼ PINTS/3 CUPS CHICKEN STOCK

SALT AND FRESHLY GROUND BLACK PEPPER

3 TBSP OLIVE OIL

2 ONIONS, THINLY SLICED

115g/4oz DICED PANCETTA

350g/12oz MIXED MUSHROOMS, LARGER ONES SLICED

2–3 GARLIC CLOVES, FINELY CHOPPED

55g/2oz/4 TBSP BUTTER

55g/2oz/½ CUP PLAIN (ALL-PURPOSE) FLOUR

115g/4oz/½ CUP MASCARPONE CHEESE

250g/9oz (6 SHEETS) FRESH LASAGNE

40g/1½oz/6 TBSP FRESHLY GRATED PARMESAN CHEESE

1. Put the chicken thighs and thyme in a saucepan, add the wine and stock, season well with salt and pepper and bring to the boil. Cover and simmer gently for 45 minutes, or until the chicken is very tender and cooked through.

2. Leave the chicken to cool. Lift out of the stock, discard the skin and take the meat off the bones. Cut the meat into bite-size pieces and set aside. Discard the thyme and strain the stock into a measuring jug. Make up to 750ml/1¼ pints/3 cups with extra water if necessary.

3. Heat 1 tbsp of the oil in a frying pan, add the onions and pancetta and cook for 5 minutes, stirring, until just beginning to turn golden. Using a slotted spoon, transfer to a plate. Add the remaining oil to the pan, heat, then add the mushrooms and garlic and cook until just beginning to colour.

4. Heat the butter in a saucepan, stir in the flour, then gradually stir in the reserved chicken stock. Bring to the boil, stirring until thickened. Whisk in the mascarpone cheese. Taste and adjust the seasoning.

Recipe continues…

To serve from frozen

Thaw overnight in the fridge. Preheat the oven to 190°C/375°F/Gas Mark 5. Remove the foil and bake for 50–60 minutes until the top is golden and the lasagne piping hot. Check after 40 minutes and cover loosely with foil if the lasagne is browning too quickly.

5. Spoon a little of the sauce into a 23cm/9in square dish that is 5cm/2in deep, add 2 lasagne sheets, then cover with half the chicken, half the onion and pancetta mixture and one-third of the mushrooms. Moisten with more sauce. Top with 2 more lasagne sheets, the rest of the chicken, onions and pancetta, then add half the remaining sauce and another one-third of the mushrooms.

6. Cover with the 2 remaining lasagne sheets, the remaining mushrooms and sauce. Sprinkle with the Parmesan.

7. To serve, cook the lasagne in an oven preheated to 190°C/375°F/Gas Mark 5, for 40–45 minutes, until the top is golden and bubbling.

BOLOGNESE SAUCE

For a classic lasagne, make a Bolognese-style sauce. Brown 500g/1lb 2oz minced beef with a chopped onion in 1 tbsp olive oil. Add 1 finely chopped garlic clove, 1 tsp dried oregano, 250ml/8fl oz/1 cup red wine and a 400g can chopped tomatoes. Cover and simmer for 30 minutes. In a separate pan, melt 55g/2oz/4 tbsp butter, stir in 55g/2oz/½ cup plain (all-purpose) flour, then gradually mix in 600ml/1 pint/2½ cups milk and bring to the boil, stirring, until thickened and smooth. Flavour with grated nutmeg, salt and pepper. Layer ½ Bolognese sauce, 2 sheets lasagne, ½ cheese sauce, 2 sheets lasagne, rest of Bolognese sauce, lasagne and cheese sauce in the dish. Add freshly grated Parmesan and bake as in step 7.

FREEZING TIP

Rather than baking this in a foil dish, you could line your favourite ovenproof dish with foil, allowing a generous overhang of foil over the top of the dish. Layer up the lasagne, then freeze until firm. Lift the lasagne out of the dish and wrap the foil over the top of the lasagne. Freeze, then peel off the foil and return the lasagne to the china dish to thaw.

To freeze
At the end of step 6, cool completely then open-freeze until the top is firm. Wrap the dish in foil, seal and label. Freeze for up to 1 month – see guidelines on the pack of pasta.

TEO CHEW-STYLE CHICKEN

This Malaysian dish is based on a soy broth flavoured with ginger, garlic, aromatic star anise and Sichuan peppercorns. It is traditionally used to braise a whole duck, but chicken or duck legs freeze successfully. Serve with rice or egg noodles and stir-fried tenderstem broccoli with chilli, tossed with soy sauce.

SERVES 4

PREP: 15 MINUTES

COOK: 1 HOUR 10 MINUTES

REHEAT FROM FROZEN: THAW OVERNIGHT,
    REHEAT 5–7 MINUTES IN THE MICROWAVE OR
    10–15 MINUTES IN A SAUCEPAN

1 TBSP SUNFLOWER OIL

900g/2lb CHICKEN THIGHS ON THE BONE, SKIN TRIMMED

1 LARGE ONION, FINELY CHOPPED

2 TSP CORNFLOUR (CORNSTARCH)

1 ORANGE: PARE THE RIND IN STRIPS WITH A VEG PRINTER
    AND SQUEEZE THE JUICE

2 GARLIC CLOVES, THINLY SLICED

5cm/2in PIECE FRESH GINGER, PEELED AND THINLY SLICED

3 STAR ANISE

300ml/½ PINT/1¼ CUPS CHICKEN STOCK

4 TBSP CHINESE RICE WINE OR DRY SHERRY

3 TBSP SOY SAUCE

1 TSP SICHUAN PEPPERCORNS, ROUGHLY CRUSHED

CHINESE EGG NOODLES, COOKED, TO SERVE

1. Preheat the oven to 180°C/350°F/Gas Mark 4. Heat the oil in a large frying pan, add the chicken and cook for about 5 minutes, until browned on both sides. Using a slotted spoon, transfer to a casserole dish.

2. Add the onion to the pan and cook for 5 minutes, stirring, until just beginning to turn golden. Mix the cornflour with the orange juice in a small bowl until smooth.

3. Add the garlic, ginger and star anise to the pan, cook for 1 minute, then stir in the stock, wine or sherry and orange juice. Add the soy sauce, peppercorns and large strips of orange rind. Bring to the boil, then pour over the chicken.

4. Cover the casserole dish and cook for 1 hour, until the chicken is cooked.

5. To serve, discard the larger pieces of orange rind and spoon into bowls of just cooked egg noodles.

TO MAKE THIS DISH WITH DUCK LEGS…

Dry fry 4 duck legs until golden, then drain off any excess duck fat, leaving just enough to fry the onions. Continue to step 4, then bake the casserole at 180°C/350°F/Gas Mark 4 for 1½ hours, or until the duck is tender and cooked through.

To serve from frozen

Thaw overnight in the fridge. Microwave individual portions for 5-7 minutes on full power or transfer to a saucepan, cover and bring to the boil, then cook over a medium heat for 15 minutes, until piping hot.

To freeze

At the end of step 4, leave to cool completely. Pack into individual serving dishes, cover, seal and label. Freeze for up to 3 months.

LET'S CELEBRATE

When a Christmas or Thanksgiving roast turkey dinner is imminent, spread the preparation by doing as much as you can in advance. You might like to serve the roast turkey with dauphinoise potatoes (see page 90) or garlicky rosemary roast potatoes (see page 18)

ALL RECIPES SERVE 8

ROAST TURKEY

PREP: 30 MINUTES, PLUS 1 HOUR STANDING
COOK FROM FROZEN: THAW ACCORDING TO INSTRUCTIONS
ON PACK; COOK 20 MINUTES PER 450G/1LB

Defrost a 4.5–5.5kg/10-12lb turkey following the instructions on the wrapper, then allow it to come to room temperature for 1 hour before preparation. Preheat the oven to 190°C/375°F/Gas Mark 5 (170°C for a fan oven). Rinse the turkey inside and out with cold water, drain well, then spoon half the stuffing into the neck end. Add ½ lemon and ½ orange to the body cavity with 1 onion and a few bay leaves. Spread 75g/3oz/6 tbsp softened butter over the bird and sprinkle with salt and pepper. Arrange 12 rashers of streaky bacon in a lattice over the breast, tucking a few bay leaves between them. Weigh and calculate the cooking time, allowing 20 minutes for every 450g/1lb total weight. Cover the turkey with foil, then roast for the calculated time, basting often. Remove the foil and bacon lattice for the last 30 minutes to brown the turkey. To test, insert a skewer through the thickest part of the thigh into the breast; the juices will run clear when it is done, or use a meat thermometer. Leave to rest for 30 minutes before carving.

TURKEY STUFFING

TO STUFF A 4.5–5.5kg/10–12lb OVEN-READY TURKEY
PREP: 20 MINUTES
COOK: 5 MINUTES

55g/2oz/4 TBSP BUTTER
1 TBSP OLIVE OIL
350g/12oz ONIONS, FINELY CHOPPED
500g/1lb 2oz GOOD-QUALITY SAUSAGE MEAT
    OR SAUSAGES WITH THEIR SKINS REMOVED
140g/5oz/3 CUPS FRESH BREADCRUMBS
1 EGG, BEATEN
SALT AND FRESHLY GROUND BLACK PEPPER
YOUR CHOSEN FLAVOURING (SEE PAGE 42)

Make this basic mix, then add your favourite flavour combination (see page 42).

1. Heat the butter and oil in a frying pan, add the onions and cook gently for 5 minutes until just beginning to turn golden. Leave to cool.

2. Stir in the sausage meat, breadcrumbs and egg and season with plenty of salt and pepper.

3. Mix in your chosen flavouring (see page 42).

4. To use fresh: press half the stuffing into the neck cavity of the turkey, then weigh the bird and calculate the cooking time. Shape the remaining stuffing into small balls. Cook the turkey for the calculated time. Add the stuffing balls to the roasting pan (or oook in a separate roasting pan with a little oil) for the last 20–30 minutes of cooking.

Selection of stuffings on the next page; add all to the pan for the last 20–30 minutes of cooking...

TURKEY STUFFING
...CONTINUED

GINGER, CRANBERRY AND ORANGE

Peel and finely chop 5cm/2in piece fresh ginger and mix into the stuffing with 75g/3oz dried cranberries, the grated zest of 1 orange and 1 tsp roughly crushed allspice berries.

PANCETTA, PARMESAN AND CHILLI

Add 2 finely chopped celery stalks and 140g/5oz finely cubed pancetta when cooking the onions. Mix in 75g/2½oz/generous ½ cup freshly grated Parmesan, ½ tsp dried crushed red chillies and a handful of chopped fresh parsley after the sausage meat, breadcrumbs, egg and seasoning.

To freeze the stuffing

Pack into a plastic bag, seal and label. Freeze for up to 1 month.

To serve from frozen

Thaw overnight in the fridge. Press half the stuffing into the neck cavity of the turkey, then weigh the bird and calculate cooking time. Shape the remaining stuffing into small balls. Cook the turkey for the calculated time. Add the stuffing balls to the roasting pan for the last 25–30 minutes of cooking.

CHESTNUT, LEEK AND BACON

Add 200g/7oz thinly sliced leek to 140g/5oz chopped onions as you fry. Cool, then add 200g/7oz vacuum-packed prepared chestnuts, roughly chopped, and 140g/5oz bacon, grilled until golden, then chopped. Season with ¼ tsp grated nutmeg and ½ tsp ground mixed spice (pumpkin pie spice).

APPLE AND SAGE

Instead of the onion, add 350g/12oz chopped leeks to the butter and oil. Add 1 large peeled, cored and diced Bramley apple to the cooked leeks and cook for 2–3 minutes. Stir in the remaining ingredients plus the grated zest of 1 lemon and a small handful of sage leaves, roughly chopped.

APRICOT, PECAN AND GARLIC

Replace the sausage meat with the same weight of herb sausages, skins removed. Stir in 115g/4oz ready-to-eat (plumped) dried apricots, chopped, 55g/2oz/½ cup pecan nuts, roughly crumbled, 2 finely chopped garlic cloves, 1 tsp roughly crushed black peppercorns and a pinch of freshly grated nutmeg.

STUFFED RED ONIONS

Instead of cooking the stuffing as small balls, halve 6 medium red onions and remove the centres with a teaspoon. Fill with half the stuffing. Pack into a foil container, brush with a little olive oil, then cover, seal and label. Freeze for up to 1 month. Thaw overnight in the fridge. Add to the turkey roasting pan for the last 45 minutes of cooking, spooning some of the turkey juices over, until the onions are soft and the stuffing is hot right through.

SAUSAGE AND BACON ROLLS

Spread a little wholegrain mustard over one side of 8 slices of bacon, cut in half and roll each half around 16 herby chipolata (small) sausages. Pack into a foil dish, cover, seal and label, then freeze. Thaw overnight in the fridge. Cook on a small baking sheet for the last 25–30 minutes of turkey cooking.

CRANBERRY SAUCE

PREP: 5 MINUTES

COOK: 10 MINUTES

REHEAT FROM THE FREEZER: THAW OVERNIGHT IN FRIDGE; REHEAT
   3 MINUTES IN MICROWAVE OR 5–6 MINUTES IN SAUCEPAN

300g/10½oz/3 CUPS CRANBERRIES

6 TBSP RUBY PORT

GRATED ZEST OF 1 SMALL ORANGE

5cm/2in PIECE CINNAMON STICK

2 SMALL STAR ANISE

75g/3oz/SCANT ½ CUP CASTER (SUPERFINE) SUGAR

Put the cranberries, port, orange zest and spices in a saucepan and cook over a low heat, stirring from time to time, until the cranberries soften.

Stir in the sugar and cook gently for 5 minutes, stirring occasionally until the sugar has dissolved. Remove the cinnamon.

To freeze the cranberry sauce

Leave to cool. Pack into a microwavable container, seal and label. Freeze for up to 2 months.

To serve from frozen

Thaw overnight in the fridge, then reheat in a small saucepan, stirring, until piping hot. Or loosen the lid and microwave on full power for 5–6 minutes, stirring twice, until hot.

To freeze the bread sauce

Pack into a container after adding the nutmeg. Dot the surface with 25g/1oz/2 tbsp butter and pour 3 tbsp double (heavy) cream over. Cover, seal, label and freeze for up to 1 month.

To serve from frozen

Thaw overnight in the fridge. Break up the block. Reheat in a small saucepan, stirring, until piping hot. Or microwave, covered, on full power for 3–4 minutes, stirring once or twice.

BREAD SAUCE

Press 4 cloves into a peeled onion and place in a saucepan with 600ml/1 pint/2½ cups milk and 2 bay leaves. Bring just to the boil, then take off the heat and leave to stand for 30 minutes. Drain and discard the onion and bay leaves. Add 115g/4oz/2½ cups fresh breadcrumbs, salt and pepper to the milk, bring to the boil and cook, stirring, for 4–5 minutes, until thickened. Take off the heat, stir in a little grated nutmeg, taste and adjust the seasoning. Leave to cool. Just before serving, reheat and stir in 25g/1oz/2 tbsp butter and 3 tbsp double (heavy) cream.

FISH

FISH

Fresh fish is best eaten or frozen on the day of purchase. It makes sense to buy double what you need, then you can cook it all, eat half for supper and stock your freezer with a dish that you can pull out at a later date when you're short of time.

Fish pie can be cooked from frozen, so it could be a lifesaver on a busy day. Thai-style fish curry, a cheat's bouillabaisse or a Greek-inspired slow-cooked squid flavoured with white wine and lemon can all be made in advance, frozen, and then defrosted before being reheated.

A bag of frozen raw fish fillets makes a versatile standby: cook from frozen with a slice of herb, chilli or olive butter, add a warm pea salad or make into a creamy gratin with leeks and spinach. When buying fish, always check the label. If it has already been frozen and thawed before sale you will need to cook it before freezing. Do not refreeze raw fish that has been thawed.

If using frozen prawns (shrimp) or mixed shellfish, follow the guidelines on the pack: most say to thaw fully before use while others give instructions for using from frozen. If you need to thaw them in a hurry, soak the bag in cold water, changing the water several times. After 30 minutes they will be ready to use. Don't be tempted to use warm water.

THAI GREEN CURRY WITH MONKFISH

Monkfish is a wonderfully firm white fish, and perfectly suited to cooking in a spicy coconut milk curry. You could also use hake, cod loins, salmon or trout fillets.

SERVES 4

PREP: 15 MINUTES

COOK: 20 MINUTES

REHEAT FROM FROZEN: THAW OVERNIGHT,
    REHEAT 8–10 MINUTES

1 ONION, QUARTERED

1 STEM OF LEMONGRASS, THICKLY SLICED

2.5cm/1in PIECE FRESH GINGER, PEELED AND
    THINLY SLICED

1 TBSP SUNFLOWER OIL

1 TBSP THAI GREEN CURRY PASTE, OR TO TASTE

400ml CAN FULL-FAT COCONUT MILK

150ml/5fl oz/⅔ CUP FISH OR VEGETABLE STOCK

GRATED ZEST AND JUICE OF 1 LIME

1–2 TSP THAI FISH SAUCE (NAM PLA)

1 TSP PALM SUGAR OR CASTER (SUPERFINE) SUGAR

600g/1lb 5oz MONKFISH FILLETS, HALVED

LARGE HANDFUL OF FRESH CORIANDER (CILANTRO) LEAVES

SMALL HANDFUL OF FRESH BASIL LEAVES

To serve

RICE NOODLES, COOKED

300g/100oz READY-PREPARED STIR-FRY VEGETABLES,
    STIR-FRIED IN A LITTLE SUNFLOWER OIL

FRESH HERBS TO GARNISH

1. Put the onion, lemongrass and ginger in a food processor or blender and blitz until very finely chopped. Heat the oil in a large saucepan and cook the onion mixture over a low heat for 5 minutes, stirring, until softened but not coloured. Stir in the curry paste and cook for 30 seconds.

2. Stir in the coconut milk, stock, lime zest and juice, fish sauce and sugar. Bring just to the boil, cover and simmer gently for 5 minutes.

3. Add the monkfish pieces in a single layer, push down into the liquid, cover and simmer gently for 8 minutes, until just cooked.

4. Using a slotted spoon, lift the fish out of the pan and slice thickly. Chop the herbs and stir into the sauce, then return the fish to the pan. Taste and add more fish sauce if liked.

5. To serve, spoon into bowls over cooked rice noodles. Top with stir-fried vegetables and garnish with fresh herbs.

To serve from frozen
Thaw overnight in the fridge. Transfer to a saucepan, cover and reheat for 10 minutes until piping hot. Serve with rice noodles, stir-fried vegetables and fresh herbs.

To freeze
At the end of step 4, leave to cool. Pack in two or single-portion freezer containers, seal and label. Freeze for up to 2 months.

CHEAT'S BOUILLABAISSE

This is a main-course soup packed with fish and seafood, delicately flavoured with saffron and white wine. Traditionally made with a mixed catch fresh from a sunny Mediterranean quayside, this version uses fish available from the supermarket: monkfish, red mullet, red snapper, cod, haddock, tilapia or hake.

SERVES 4

PREP: 20 MINUTES

COOK: 40 MINUTES

COOK FROM FROZEN: THAW OVERNIGHT,
    REHEAT 8–10 MINUTES

2 TBSP OLIVE OIL

1 LARGE ONION, FINELY CHOPPED

2 CELERY STALKS, FINELY CHOPPED

2 GARLIC CLOVES, FINELY CHOPPED

1 RED PEPPER, DESEEDED AND ROUGHLY CHOPPED

500g/1lb 2oz TOMATOES (PEELED IF YOU LIKE),
    ROUGHLY CHOPPED

250ml/8fl oz/1 CUP DRY WHITE WINE

250ml/8fl oz/1 CUP FISH STOCK

1 TBSP TOMATO PURÉE (TOMATO PASTE)

2 SPRIGS OF FRESH THYME

2 SPRIGS OF FRESH TARRAGON

LARGE PINCH OF SAFFRON THREADS

SALT AND FRESHLY GROUND BLACK PEPPER

500g/1lb 2oz WHITE FISH FILLETS (USE A MIXTURE
    OF FISH OR JUST ONE TYPE)

350g/12oz FROZEN MIXED SEAFOOD (SLICED SQUID
    RINGS, MUSSELS AND PRAWNS), THAWED ONLY IF
    SERVING THE DISH NOW, CLEANED

1 SMALL BAGUETTE, TO SERVE

ROUILLE, TO SERVE (SEE PAGE 52)

1. Heat the oil in a saucepan, add the onion and celery and cook gently for 10 minutes, stirring from time to time until softened and just turning golden. Stir in the garlic, red pepper and tomatoes and cook for 2–3 minutes.

2. Stir in the wine, stock and tomato purée. Add the herbs and saffron and season generously with salt and pepper. Bring to the boil, cover and simmer gently for 15 minutes.

3. Add the fish fillets in a single layer if possible, cover the pan and cook gently for 10 minutes or until the fish is just cooked. Lift out onto a plate, remove any skin and bones, break into large flakes and return to the soup.

4. To serve, discard any mussels that fail to close when tapped against the side of the sink. Add the thawed seafood to the soup and reheat for 5 minutes, until the seafood is piping hot. Discard any mussels that have failed to open. Slice and toast the baguette. Serve the bouillabaisse in shallow bowls, with toast and a spoonful of rouille (see page 52).

Recipe continues…

To serve from frozen

Thaw overnight in the fridge. Reheat the bouillabaisse in a saucepan, stirring gently until piping hot throughout. Toast the baguette slices. Serve with the rouille.

To freeze

At the end of step 3, leave to cool completely. Pack into 4 containers, divide the frozen seafood between the containers then cover, seal and label. Freeze for up to 2 months. Slice and open-freeze the baguette, then pack into a plastic bag.

BOUILLABAISSE
...CONTINUED

ROUILLE

Take 3 roasted red peppers from a jar, drain and place in a food processor or blender. Add a large pinch of saffron threads, soaked in 1 tbsp boiling water for 5 minutes, 3 finely chopped garlic cloves, 3 tbsp olive oil, a halved and deseeded red chilli, and a slice of bread, torn up. Blitz until smooth.

To freeze the rouille
Spoon into an ice-cube tray, freeze until firm, then transfer to a plastic bag.

To serve the rouille from frozen
Thaw as many cubes as you need in a dish. Stir before serving.

SALMON.
ASPARAGUS AND PEA
RISOTTO

SERVES 4

PREP: 15 MINUTES

COOK: 35 MINUTES

REHEAT FROM FROZEN: 8–10 MINUTES IN THE MICROWAVE
OR 30–35 MINUTES IN THE OVEN

25g/1oz/2 TBSP BUTTER

1 TBSP OLIVE OIL

1 ONION, FINELY CHOPPED

2 CELERY STALKS, FINELY CHOPPED

850ml–1.2 LITRES/1½–2 PINTS/3½–5 CUPS FISH
OR VEGETABLE STOCK

225g/8oz/1¼ CUPS ARBORIO RICE

GRATED ZEST OF 1 UNWAXED LEMON

2 GARLIC CLOVES, FINELY CHOPPED

175ml/6fl oz/¾ CUP DRY WHITE WINE

450g/1lb SALMON FILLET, CUT INTO 4 PIECES

SALT AND FRESHLY GROUND BLACK PEPPER

250g/9oz ASPARAGUS, TRIMMED

4 TBSP FRESHLY GRATED PARMESAN CHEESE,
PLUS EXTRA TO SERVE

4 TBSP CRÈME FRAÎCHE

115g/4oz/SCANT 1 CUP FROZEN PEAS

Individual portions of risotto can be quickly reheated for a luxurious supper. Adding extra stock to the risotto before freezing ensures that it is soft and creamy when reheated.

1. Heat the butter and oil in a large frying pan, add the onion and celery and cook gently for 5 minutes, stirring from time to time until softened but not browned. Bring the stock to the boil in a saucepan.

2. Stir the rice, lemon zest and garlic into the onion mixture and cook for 1 minute, until the rice is glossy. Add the wine and 2 ladlefuls of hot stock, then arrange the salmon on top. Season well. Cover and simmer for 10 minutes, adding stock as needed, until the salmon is just cooked, then lift out onto a plate.

3. Cook the risotto for a further 15 minutes or so, uncovered, adding more hot stock as it is absorbed until you have added about 850ml/1½ pints/3½ cups, and stirring frequently, until the rice is soft and creamy.

4. Meanwhile, cook the asparagus in boiling water for 2 minutes. Drain and cool quickly under cold running water or in a bowl of iced water and drain again.

5. Discard the salmon skin and bones and break the flesh into large flakes. Stir the Parmesan into the risotto and adjust the seasoning.

6. Add the salmon, crème fraîche and peas to the risotto, top with the asparagus, cover and cook for 3 minutes until the peas and salmon are hot, adding a little extra stock if needed. To serve, spoon into shallow bowls and sprinkle with a little extra Parmesan.

To serve from frozen

Microwave one portion at a time, with the lid slightly loosened, for 8-10 minutes on full power, stirring twice. If using foil dishes, preheat the oven to 190°C/375°F/ Gas Mark 5 and reheat the risotto in the oven for 30-35 minutes. Serve with grated Parmesan.

To freeze

At the end of step 5, leave the risotto to cool. Divide among 4 microwavable or foil containers. Divide the salmon between the containers, add the crème fraîche, asparagus and frozen peas (not thawed). Pour the remaining, now cold, stock around the edges of the containers. Cover, seal and label. Freeze for up to 2 months.

FISH PIE

Fish pie is one of those comforting dishes that is lovely to eat, but creates a lot of washing up. Making one to eat now and one to freeze for later uses the same amount of pans and is almost as quick to prepare. It can be baked from frozen.

SERVES 8
PREP: 30 MINUTES
COOK: 45–50 MINUTES
COOK FROM FROZEN: 1¼ HOURS

1 LITRE/¾ PINT/4 CUPS SEMI-SKIMMED (LOW-FAT) MILK
2 BAY LEAVES
LARGE PINCH OF MACE PIECES
1 ONION, QUARTERED
SALT AND FRESHLY GROUND BLACK PEPPER
225g/8oz SMOKED COD FILLET
300g/10oz UNSMOKED COD FILLET
680g/1½lb SALMON FILLET, CUT INTO 4 PIECES
250g/9oz RAW PEELED PRAWNS (SHRIMP), THAWED IF FROZEN
1.25kg/2lb 12oz POTATOES, PEELED AND THINLY SLICED
LARGE HANDFUL OF FRESH PARSLEY, FINELY CHOPPED
110g/4oz/8 TBSP BUTTER
115g/4oz/1 CUP PLAIN (ALL-PURPOSE) FLOUR
90ml/3fl oz/6 TBSP NOILLY PRAT OR DRY WHITE WINE
150ml/5fl oz/⅔ CUP FISH STOCK MADE WITH ½ A GOOD-QUALITY FISH STOCK CUBE
40g/1½oz BROWN CRABMEAT (OPTIONAL)
55g/2oz CHEDDAR OR GRUYÈRE CHEESE, FINELY GRATED

1. Put the milk in a large saucepan, add the bay leaves, mace, onion and plenty of salt and pepper. Bring slowly to the boil, then add the smoked and unsmoked cod and salmon pieces. Bring the milk back to the boil, cover and simmer gently for 5 minutes.

2. Add the prawns and push down into the milk, cover the pan and cook gently for 3–4 minutes until they are pink and the pieces of fish break easily into flakes.

3. Meanwhile, bring another large saucepan of water to the boil, add the potato slices. Cook for 3–5 minutes, until just tender. Drain into a colander and cool quickly under a cold tap, drain and leave to cool.

4. Using a slotted spoon, lift the fish and prawns onto a large plate; pour any milk that collects on the plate back into the pan. Skin and flake the fish fillets, discarding any bones. Divide the fish between two 23cm/9in square, 5cm/2in deep, foil dishes and sprinkle with the parsley. Strain the milk into a large jug, discarding the bay, mace and onion.

Recipe continues...

FISH PIE
...CONTINUED

5. Melt the butter in the cleaned potato pan, then whisk in the flour and cook for 30 seconds. Gradually whisk in the milk, Noilly Prat or wine and stock and bring slowly to the boil, whisking continuously until thickened and smooth. Whisk in the strained crabmeat, if using. Pour just under two-thirds of the sauce over the fish in the dishes.

6. Arrange the cooked potato slices randomly, but overlapping, over the sauce. Drizzle the remaining sauce over the top, then sprinkle with the cheese.

7. To serve, cook in an oven preheated to 190°C/375°F/Gas 5 for 30–35 minutes until golden and piping hot.

ALSO TRY
Vary the types of fish using a mixture of your choice or all one kind. Roughly chopped hard-boiled egg may also be added. Frozen fish fillets can be added to the milk but will need to be cooked for 10 minutes before the defrosted prawns are added.

To freeze
At the end of step 6, loosely cover the dishes with lids or foil, leaving a little space for the steam to escape, and leave to cool. Seal and label. Freeze for up to 2 months.

To serve from frozen
Preheat the oven to 190°C/ 375°F/Gas 5. Remove the lid or foil from each pie and cook from frozen for 1¼ hours, until piping hot and the top is golden. Check after 30–40 minutes and loosely cover if it's browning too quickly.

SMOKED MACKEREL AND WATERCRESS FISH CAKES

Mackerel is rather under-used, yet it is sustainable and inexpensive. These fish cakes could also be made with lightly steamed salmon, trout fillets or smoked haddock.

MAKES 8 FISH CAKES
PREP: 25 MINUTES
COOK: 15 MINUTES
TO FINISH: 10 MINUTES
COOK FROM FROZEN: 30–35 MINUTES

500g/1lb 2oz POTATOES, CUT INTO CHUNKS
4 EGGS
25g/1oz/2 TBSP BUTTER
SALT
225g/8oz PEPPERED SMOKED MACKEREL FILLETS,
    SKINNED AND FLAKED
4 SPRING ONIONS (SCALLIONS), FINELY CHOPPED
LARGE HANDFUL OF WATERCRESS, ROUGHLY CHOPPED
85g/3oz/2 CUPS FRESH WHITE BREADCRUMBS
OLIVE OIL

To serve

GREEK-STYLE YOGURT OR CRÈME FRAÎCHE, FLAVOURED WITH
    HORSERADISH SAUCE
GREEN SALAD
LEMON WEDGES

1. Cook the potatoes in a saucepan of boiling water for 15 minutes, until tender.

2. Meanwhile, put 2 eggs in a saucepan, cover with cold water, bring to the boil, then simmer for 8 minutes. Drain, rinse with cold water to cool quickly, then tap the shells against the side of the pan, peel and roughly chop.

3. Drain the potatoes and mash with the butter and a little salt. Add the fish, chopped hardboiled eggs, spring onions and watercress. Divide the mixture into 8 mounds and leave to cool for 15 minutes.

4. Beat the remaining 2 eggs in a shallow dish and tip the breadcrumbs onto a plate. Pat the mackerel mounds into neat cakes of about 7.5cm/3in diameter. Dip the fish cakes in the beaten egg to coat on both sides. Using a fish slice or two forks, transfer them to the breadcrumbs, coat all over, then place on a baking sheet.

Recipe continues…

MAKE YOUR OWN BREADCRUMBS
Don't throw away leftover bread: trim off the crusts and cut the bread into cubes, then blitz in a food processor or blender to make fine breadcrumbs. Pack into a plastic bag or container, seal and label. Freeze for up to 3 months. For fish cakes, use the crumbs while still frozen, then transfer the fish cakes to the freezer before they thaw.

FISH CAKES
...CONTINUED

5. Leave to cool, then chill in the fridge for 1 hour to firm up. Heat 2 tbsp of oil in a large frying pan over a medium heat and cook the fish cakes for 5 minutes on each side, adding a little extra oil if needed, until golden and piping hot. Serve with yogurt or crème fraîche flavoured with horseradish sauce, salad leaves and lemon wedges.

To freeze

At the end of step 4, cover the fish cakes loosely with clingfilm (plastic wrap) or foil and leave to cool. Freeze on the baking sheet until firm, then stack in a plastic container, interleaving with squares of baking parchment so that they don't stick together. Seal and label. Freeze for up to 1 month.

To serve from frozen

Preheat the oven to 200°C/400°F/Gas Mark 6. Put as many fish cakes as you need on a baking sheet sprayed with olive oil. Spray the tops of the fish cakes with more oil, then bake for 20 minutes. Turn over, spray with oil again and bake for 10-15 minutes until golden and piping hot.

4 QUICK WAYS
WITH FROZEN FISH

A bag of frozen fish fillets is a great standby for an easy midweek meal. There's no need to thaw them first, just cook in a hot oven. Salmon, trout, cod, smoked haddock or other fish can be used if preferred. Fish fillets vary in size, so check the pack before buying. If small, you might want to cook 2 fillets per portion, keeping all the other ingredients the same.

CHINESE-STYLE BAKED FISH

SERVES 4
PREP: 10 MINUTES
COOK: 25–30 MINUTES

Preheat the oven to 190°C/375°F/Gas Mark 5. Cut 4 large pieces of baking parchment and fold in half. Cut 2 carrots and 3 spring onions (scallions) into matchsticks and divide among the pieces of paper. Add 250g/9oz trimmed asparagus and 115g/4oz trimmed green beans. Add a 140g/5oz frozen salmon or cod fillet to each piece of baking parchment, divide a 4cm/1½in piece of peeled and finely chopped fresh ginger, 1 sliced small green chilli, 2 tbsp light soy sauce, 2 tbsp dry Sherry and a little torn coriander (cilantro) between parcels, fold up and seal edges well. Tie with string. Cook on a baking sheet in the oven for 25–30 minutes, until cooked. Serve with boiled rice.

COD WITH LENTILS AND MEDITERRANEAN VEG

SERVES 4
PREP: 10 MINUTES
COOK: 35 MINUTES

Preheat the oven to 180°C/350°F/Gas Mark 4. Brush a roasting pan with a little olive oil, then add 450g/1lb peeled and deseeded butternut squash, cut into 1cm/½in dice. Roast for 10 minutes.

Turn the squash and push to the edges of the roasting pan. Drain 2 x 400g cans of green lentils, rinse and drain again, then mound up in the centre of the roasting pan. Drizzle with 4 tsp balsamic vinegar and mix in 2 finely chopped garlic cloves and a little salt and pepper. Arrange 300g/10oz/2 cups halved cherry tomatoes and 2 small red onions, cut into wedges, around the edge of the roasting pan. Put 4 x 140g/5oz frozen cod fillets on top of the lentils. Mix 2 tsp harissa paste with 3 tbsp olive oil, drizzle over the fish and vegetables. Roast for 25 minutes until the fish and squash are cooked. If the veggies need a little longer, take the fish out and wrap in foil. To serve, spoon into bowls and sprinkle with a little chopped parsley or coriander (cilantro).

FLAVOURED BUTTERS

Make a spiced butter by mixing a little chopped fresh chilli or a sprinkling of dried crushed chillies, finely chopped fresh coriander (cilantro) and some grated unwaxed lemon zest into 115g/4oz/½ cup softened butter. Or mix in 2 finely chopped garlic cloves and a small bunch of finely chopped mixed herbs. For olive butter, mix in 55g/2oz pitted chopped olives, the grated zest of 1 lemon and a small bunch of fresh chopped basil. Shape into a log, slice and freeze slices interleaved with small squares of baking parchment in a plastic container. Take out as many as you need and add to frozen fish fillets, wrap in foil and bake in the oven. Or add to the top of a pan-fried or grilled fish fillet, or even a steak or lamb chop, for a quick burst of flavour. Freeze for up to 3 months.

EASY FISH GRATIN

SERVES 4
PREP: 10 MINUTES
COOK: 30 MINUTES

Preheat the oven to 180°C/350°F/Gas Mark 4. Melt 25g/1oz/2 tbsp butter in a frying pan, add 225g/8oz thinly sliced leeks and cook for 2 minutes. Add 115g/4oz rinsed and drained spinach and cook for 1 minute until just wilted. Season with a little grated nutmeg, salt and pepper, then mix together and spoon into a shallow ovenproof dish. Arrange 4 x 140g/5oz frozen smoked haddock fillets on top so that they fit snugly side by side.

Mix 250ml/8fl oz/1 cup double (heavy) cream with 115g/4oz grated Cheddar or Gruyère cheese and a little salt and pepper, spoon over the fish and sprinkle with 2 tbsp fresh or frozen breadcrumbs. Bake for 25–30 minutes, until the sauce is bubbling and the fish cooked through. Grill for 1–2 minutes if needed to lightly brown the top. Serve with salad.

ROASTED SALMON WITH WARM PEA SALAD

SERVES 4
PREP: 10 MINUTES
COOK: 25–30 MINUTES

Preheat the oven to 180°C/350°F/Gas Mark 4. Arrange 4 x 140g/5oz frozen salmon fillets in an oiled roasting pan, drizzle with a little olive oil and sprinkle with salt and freshly ground black pepper. Roast for 25–30 minutes or until the fish is just cooked and can be easily broken into flakes.

Toward the end of the cooking time heat 1 tbsp olive oil in a frying pan, add 3 chopped spring onions (scallions) and 3 deseeded chopped tomatoes and cook for 1 minute until just softened. Add 225g/8oz/generous 1½ cups frozen peas (no need to thaw first) and cook gently for 3 minutes, stirring until thawed. Slice 2 Little Gem (or 1 Boston) lettuce, add to the peas and cook for 30 seconds, then spoon onto plates and top with the salmon.

LEMON SQUID
AND POTATO SALAD
WITH SALSA VERDE

Inspired by the Greek squid casseroles that are cooked long and slow with red wine, this version is gently cooked with lemon, new potatoes and wine and perfumed with Mediterranean rosemary and bay. Serve hot or slightly warm, with crisp salad leaves. Try with red wine instead of white and serve with garlic bread.

SERVES 4

PREP: 15 MINUTES

COOK: 2 HOURS

REHEAT FROM FROZEN: THAW OVERNIGHT AND REHEAT IN A SAUCEPAN FOR 8–10 MINUTES

400g/14oz CLEANED AND PREPARED SQUID, THAWED IF FROZEN

2 TBSP OLIVE OIL

2 LARGE ONIONS, THINLY SLICED

175ml/6fl oz/¾ CUP FISH STOCK

175ml/6fl oz/¾ CUP DRY WHITE WINE

2–3 SPRIGS OF FRESH ROSEMARY

2 BAY LEAVES

SALT AND FRESHLY GROUND BLACK PEPPER

400g/14oz BABY NEW POTATOES, SCRUBBED AND THINLY SLICED

1 LEMON, THINLY SLICED

SALAD LEAVES AND SALSA VERDE TO SERVE

1. Preheat the oven to 160°C/325°F/Gas Mark 3. Put the squid tentacles into a colander and rinse with cold water. Rinse the squid tubes inside and out and drain. Thickly slice the squid tubes and trim the base of the tentacles if necessary.

2. Heat the oil in a frying pan, add the onions and cook gently for 5 minutes, stirring occasionally, until just beginning to turn golden. Add the fish stock, wine, herbs, salt and pepper and bring to the boil.

3. Arrange the sliced potatoes in an ovenproof dish, top with the squid, then pour the onion mixture over. Arrange the lemon slices over the surface, then push down into the liquid, using a fork. Cover and cook in the oven for 2 hours.

4. Serve warm, over salad leaves, topped with salsa verde.

To freeze

At the end of step 3, leave the squid casserole to cool completely. Pack into individual foil containers, seal and label. Freeze for up to 2 months.

To serve from frozen

Thaw completely overnight in the fridge. Reheat in a saucepan for 8-10 minutes until piping hot. Serve over salad leaves and spoon the salsa verde over the top.

SALSA VERDE

Finely chop a handful of fresh parsley, 4 drained anchovy fillets (optional), 2 garlic cloves and 2 tsp drained capers, then mix in a bowl with 2 tbsp olive oil and freshly ground black pepper to taste.

To freeze the salsa verde

Pack the salsa verde into individual foil parcels. Seal and label. Freeze for up to 1 month.

To serve the salsa verde from frozen
Thaw overnight in the fridge. Stir before serving.

VEG

VEG

Make the most of a bumper homegrown harvest or special offers from your local market or pick-your-own farm. Prepare, blanch and freeze vegetables for a store of quick, healthy side dishes at a moment's notice, or make creamy potatoes dauphinoise for a luxurious supper. Try a heartwarming beetroot and horseradish or spiced lentil and squash soup, a crisp vegetable tart, a fragrant red wine casserole, or a batch of brilliantly versatile slow-cooked tomato sauce.

To freeze vegetables on their own rather than as part of a recipe, they must first be blanched (cooked briefly in a saucepan of boiling water) to preserve their colour and flavour.

To blanch, two-thirds-fill your largest saucepan with water and bring to a rolling boil. Plunge no more than 500g/1lb 2oz prepared vegetables into the water, ideally in a blanching basket at one time.

Bring back to the boil as quickly as possible, and cook as follows:
• 1 minute for fleshy or tender vegetables such as peas, sliced courgettes (zucchini), mangetout (snow peas) or spinach
• 2 minutes for asparagus and sliced peppers
• 3 minutes for Brussels sprouts, broccoli or cauliflower florets, broad (fava) beans, runner (string) and green beans
• 4–8 minutes for firm vegetables, such as corn cobs, baby beetroot (beets) or carrots

Lift the vegetables out of the water and plunge into a large bowl of cold water with ice-cubes or a frozen picnic cool block. Drain, then tip on to a tray lined with a clean tea-towel to dry. Pack portions into plastic bags, pressing out as much air as possible, then seal and label.

Don't blanch too many vegetables at a time: the water will take longer to come back to the boil and the vegetables are likely to be overcooked when you come to reheat them.

SOUP QUARTET

Soups freeze well. Freeze in individual portions and thaw in the microwave or in a saucepan on the stove for a quick and easy lunch. If you have a microwave at work you can put the frozen block of soup in a bowl and leave it on your desk to thaw. At lunchtime, give it a blast in the microwave and serve with a bread roll or apple and cheese scones (see page 104).

To serve from frozen
Put individual bag of soup in a bowl. Remove metal tie and microwave for 3 minutes on full power. Tip out of the bag into the bowl, break up, cover the bowl and microwave for 4-7 minutes more, depending on the type of soup, stirring once or twice until piping hot.

To freeze
Cover and leave to cool. Pack in individual plastic bags. Seal and label. Freeze for up to 2 months.

LETTUCE AND GARDEN HERB SOUP

A great recipe to make if your garden lettuces have grown a little too large and begun to bolt. Delicious served with a hot toasted sandwich (see page 91) or sprinkled with crisp croûtons.

SERVES 4	
PREP: 15 MINUTES	
COOK: 25–30 MINUTES	
REHEAT FROM FROZEN: 7–8 MINUTES IN THE MICROWAVE OR 15–20 MINUTES IN A SAUCEPAN	

55g/2oz/4 TBSP BUTTER
1 ONION, ROUGHLY CHOPPED
1 MEDIUM BAKING POTATO, CUBED
1 LITRE/1¾ PINTS/4 CUPS VEGETABLE, HAM OR CHICKEN STOCK
SALT AND FRESHLY GROUND BLACK PEPPER
1 ROUND LETTUCE, TORN INTO PIECES
55g/2oz FRESH PARSLEY, CHIVES AND/OR BASIL, ROUGHLY CHOPPED

1. Melt the butter in a saucepan, add the onion and cook gently for 5 minutes, until softened but not browned. Stir in the potato, then cover and cook gently for 10 minutes, stirring from time to time so that the potato doesn't stick.

2. Pour in the stock and season with salt and pepper. Bring to the boil, cover and simmer for 10 minutes until the potatoes are cooked.

3. Add the lettuce and herbs and cook for 1 minute until the lettuce has just wilted. Blend, in batches, until smooth. Taste and adjust the seasoning. Freeze or reheat if serving now.

To serve from frozen
Reheat for 7-8 minutes per portion in a covered bowl in the microwave on full power, stirred several times. Or 15-20 minutes per portion in a covered saucepan, stirring until piping hot.

SOUP QUARTET
...CONTINUED

To freeze
At the end of step 3, cover and leave to cool. Pack in individual portions. Seal and label. Freeze for up to 3 months.

To serve from frozen
Reheat for 7–8 minutes per portion in the microwave in a covered bowl on full power or 15–20 minutes per portion in a covered saucepan, stirring from time to time until piping hot.

BEETROOT AND HORSERADISH SOUP

Serve this deep, warming soup just as it is, or swirled with a spoonful of crème fraîche or Greek-style yogurt and some crispy grilled bacon or snipped fresh dill or chives. You might like to vary the flavour with the grated zest and juice of 1 orange and 1 tsp fennel seeds, or replace the horseradish with a large peeled and diced cooking apple instead.

SERVES 4

PREP: 20 MINUTES

COOK: 45 MINUTES

REHEAT FROM FROZEN: 7–8 MINUTES IN THE MICROWAVE
    OR 15–20 MINUTES IN A SAUCEPAN

55g/2oz/4 TBSP BUTTER
1 ONION, ROUGHLY CHOPPED
500g/1lb 2oz RAW BEETROOT (BEETS), TRIMMED, PEELED AND CUBED
1 LITRE/1¾ PINTS/4 CUPS VEGETABLE OR CHICKEN STOCK
40g/1½oz/4½ TBSP LONG-GRAIN WHITE RICE
2 TBSP RED WINE VINEGAR
2 TSP LIGHT BROWN SUGAR
2 TSP HORSERADISH SAUCE
1 BAY LEAF
SALT AND FRESHLY GROUND BLACK PEPPER

1. Melt the butter in a saucepan, add the onion and cook gently for 5 minutes, until softened. Stir in the beetroot, then cover and cook for 10 minutes, stirring from time to time so that the beetroot doesn't stick.

2. Pour in the stock, then stir in the rice, vinegar, sugar and horseradish sauce, add the bay leaf and season with salt and pepper. Bring to the boil, cover and simmer for 30 minutes.

3. Discard the bay leaf, then purée in batches. Taste and adjust the seasoning. Freeze or reheat if serving now.

SPICED LENTIL AND SQUASH SOUP

Gently spiced for a mellow flavoured soup. Serve with warmed naan breads (see page 103) or sprinkle with some croûtons.

SERVES 4
PREP: 20 MINUTES
COOK: 50–60 MINUTES
REHEAT FROM FROZEN: 7–8 MINUTES IN THE MICROWAVE OR 15–20 MINUTES IN A SAUCEPAN

1 TBSP SUNFLOWER OIL
1 ONION, FINELY CHOPPED
4 TSP MEDIUM CURRY PASTE
1 TSP CUMIN SEEDS, ROUGHLY CRUSHED
2 GARLIC CLOVES, FINELY CHOPPED
450g/1lb BUTTERNUT SQUASH (ABOUT ½ MEDIUM SQUASH)
    OR A LARGE WEDGE OF PUMPKIN, PEELED, DESEEDED AND CUBED
1 DESSERT APPLE, QUARTERED, CORED, PEELED AND CUBED
1.2 LITRES/2 PINTS/5 CUPS VEGETABLE OR
    CHICKEN STOCK
40g/1½oz/4 TBSP SULTANAS (GOLDEN RAISINS)
55g/2oz/5 TBSP RED LENTILS
SALT AND FRESHLY GROUND BLACK PEPPER
SMALL HANDFUL OF FRESH CORIANDER (CILANTRO), ROUGHLY CHOPPED

1. Heat the oil in a saucepan, add the onion and cook gently for 5 minutes, until softened. Stir in the curry paste, cumin seeds and garlic and cook for 1 minute, then stir in the cubed squash or pumpkin and apple.

2. Add the stock, sultanas and lentils and season generously with salt and pepper. Bring to the boil, cover and simmer gently for 45–50 minutes, until the lentils are soft.

3. Mash or purée half the soup, then taste and adjust the seasoning. Freeze, or stir in the coriander and reheat.

To serve from frozen
Reheat for 7–8 minutes per portion in the microwave in a covered bowl on full power or 15–20 minutes per portion in a covered saucepan, stirring from time to time until piping hot. Stir in the coriander and serve.

To freeze
Cover and leave to cool. Pack in individual portions. Seal and label. Freeze for up to 3 months.

To serve from frozen

Reheat in the microwave on full power for 3 minutes per portion, until partly thawed. Transfer to a serving bowl, stir, cover and microwave on full power for 4-7 minutes, stir again, until piping hot. Or put the frozen soup in a saucepan, cover and heat gently for 15-20 minutes, stirring and breaking up with a spoon and increasing the heat as the soup thaws. Serve piping hot, sprinkled with parsley or chives.

To freeze

Cover and leave to cool. Pack in individual portions. Seal and label. Freeze for up to 3 months.

WINTER VEGETABLE AND BARLEY SOUP

This classic chunky Scotch broth goes well with a toasted cheese sandwich (see page 91).

SERVES 4
PREP: 20 MINUTES
COOK: 1 HOUR 20 MINUTES
REHEAT FROM FROZEN: 7–8 MINUTES IN THE MICROWAVE OR 15–20 MINUTES IN A SAUCEPAN

55g/2oz/4 TBSP BUTTER
1 ONION, FINELY CHOPPED
1 LEEK, SLICED, WHITE AND GREEN SLICES KEPT SEPARATE
3 MEDIUM CARROTS, CUBED
½ SMALL SWEDE (RUTABAGA), CUBED
1 MEDIUM PARSNIP, CUBED
1.3 LITRES/2¼ PINTS/5½ CUPS VEGETABLE OR
    CHICKEN STOCK
40g/1½oz/¼ CUP PEARL BARLEY
3 SPRIGS OF FRESH SAGE
SALT AND FRESHLY GROUND BLACK PEPPER
HANDFUL OF FRESH PARSLEY OR CHIVES, FINELY CHOPPED

1. Melt the butter in a saucepan, add the onion and white leek slices and cook gently for 5 minutes, until softened. Stir in the diced root vegetables, cover and cook gently for 5 minutes.

2. Pour in the stock, add the barley, sage and plenty of salt and pepper. Bring to the boil, cover and simmer for 1 hour, until the barley is tender.

3. Add the green leek slices and cook for 5 minutes. Discard the sage. Taste and adjust the seasoning. Freeze, or sprinkle the soup with parsley or chives and serve hot.

SLOW-COOKED TOMATO SAUCE

Homemade tomato sauce, cooked long and slow, has a depth and intensity that can make even a humble bowl of spaghetti into something special. Make up a large batch of sauce, then split it into smaller portions and serve with pasta, or cook with mushrooms, meatballs, minced (ground) beef, diced chicken or canned tuna.

MAKES 1.5 LITRES/2¾ PINTS/6½ CUPS	
PREP: 10 MINUTES	
COOK: 1 HOUR 15 MINUTES	
REHEAT FROM FROZEN: 15–20 MINUTES IN THE MICROWAVE OR 10 MINUTES IN A SAUCEPAN	

3 TBSP OLIVE OIL
450g/1lb ONIONS, FINELY CHOPPED
4 GARLIC CLOVES, FINELY CHOPPED
1kg/2lb 4oz TOMATOES, PEELED IF YOU LIKE, ROUGHLY CHOPPED
500g/1lb 2oz/2 CUPS PASSATA (STRAINED TOMATOES)
150ml/¼ PINT /⅔ CUP RED WINE OR VEGETABLE STOCK
LARGE HANDFUL OF FRESH BASIL
1 TBSP CASTER (SUPERFINE) SUGAR
4 TSP BALSAMIC VINEGAR
SALT AND FRESHLY GROUND BLACK PEPPER

1. Heat the oil in a large saucepan, add the onions and cook gently for 10 minutes, stirring from time to time, until softened and just beginning to turn golden.

2. Add the garlic and tomatoes and cook gently for 5 minutes. Stir in the passata, wine or stock, half the basil, the sugar and balsamic vinegar. Season generously with salt and pepper and bring to the boil, stirring. Cover and cook gently for about 1 hour, stirring from time to time, until thick.

3. Discard the basil sprigs. Finely chop the leaves of the remaining basil and stir into the sauce.

To serve from frozen

Thaw one portion at a time in the microwave on full power for 6-7 minutes, stirring and breaking up once or twice until hot. Or thaw in a covered saucepan over a low heat, stirring and breaking up the block. When thawed, increase the heat until piping hot, about 10 minutes. Serve with one of the recipes on pages 77-79.

To freeze
Leave to cool. Pack into 4 containers, seal and label. Freeze for up to 3 months.

AUBERGINE PARMIGIANA

SERVES 2

TO FINISH: 35–40 MINUTES

Slice 2 medium aubergines (eggplants), arrange on a grill rack and brush lightly with olive oil (you will need about 3–4 tbsp in total). Grill under a medium-high heat for 5 minutes, until just turning golden. Turn and lightly brush the second side with oil, then grill for another 3–4 minutes. Arrange half the aubergine slices in an ovenproof dish.

Preheat the oven to 200°C/400°F/ Gas Mark 6. Thaw and reheat one portion of tomato sauce. Spoon half the sauce over the aubergines in the dish. Dice 140g/5oz mozzarella, sprinkle half over the sauce, together with 2 tbsp freshly grated Parmesan. Cover with the remaining aubergines, tomato sauce, mozzarella and another 2 tbsp grated Parmesan. Bake for 20–25 minutes until bubbling and golden. Serve with salad and garlic bread.

SPAGHETTI AL POMODORO

SERVES 2

TO FINISH: 10–15 MINUTES

Bring a large saucepan of salted water to the boil, add 175g/6oz dried spaghetti and cook for 6–8 minutes, or until al dente. Drain. Thaw and reheat one portion of tomato sauce, stir in the pasta, spoon into bowls and sprinkle with freshly grated Parmesan.

SPAGHETTI WITH MEATBALLS

Cook spaghetti as above. Cook 350g/12oz ready-made meatballs in 1 tbsp olive oil in a frying pan for 10 minutes, until browned all over. Drain off any excess oil, then add one portion of reheated tomato sauce, cover and cook for 5–10 minutes, until the meatballs are cooked through. Toss with cooked spaghetti and sprinkle with freshly grated Parmesan.

TOMATO SAUCE
...CONTINUED

SPINACH AND TOMATO GNOCCHI

SERVES 2

TO FINISH: 6–7 MINUTES

Cook 500g/1lb 2oz gnocchi in a large saucepan of boiling salted water for 3–4 minutes or until they have risen to the surface. Drain into a colander and dry the pan. Thaw and reheat one portion of tomato sauce, add 2 large handfuls of washed spinach and cook for 3 minutes, stirring until the spinach has just wilted and the sauce is hot. Add the drained gnocchi and toss gently. Spoon into bowls and sprinkle with freshly grated Parmesan.

CHICKEN ARRABIATA

SERVES 2

TO FINISH: 20 MINUTES

Thaw and reheat one portion of tomato sauce. Cut 300g/10oz (2 medium) chicken breasts into cubes. Cook in 1 tbsp olive oil for 5 minutes until browned. Add 1 deseeded and diced red pepper and cook for 5 minutes. Stir in ½ tsp dried crushed red chillies and the tomato sauce, cover and simmer for 5 minutes, or until the chicken is cooked. Meanwhile, cook 175g/6oz dried penne pasta in boiling salted water for 10–12 minutes until tender, then drain. Mix with the hot tomato sauce and serve, garnished with a handful of rocket (arugula) leaves.

EASY PEASY PASTA SAUCES

Make the most of summer vegetable gluts and freeze homegrown produce or market bargains in these simple sauces. After thawing, add to pasta for a quick family supper. To serve without freezing: reheat the sauces; cook 350–450g/12–16oz dried pasta in boiling water, drain and stir into the sauce.

PEA AND ROCKET (ARUGULA) PESTO

SERVES 4

PREP: 10 MINUTES

COOK: 1 MINUTE

REHEAT FROM FROZEN: THAW 2 HOURS, REHEAT
    5 MINUTES IN THE MICROWAVE OR 5–7 MINUTES
    IN A SAUCEPAN

Add 175g/6oz/1 generous cup shelled peas to a saucepan of boiling water, bring back to the boil and cook for 1 minute. Drain into a colander and cool quickly in ice-cold water. Drain again then add to a food processor with 8 tbsp olive oil, 25g/1oz or 2 handfulls rocket (arugula), 55g/2oz freshly grated Parmesan, 2 large handfuls of fresh basil and plenty of salt and pepper. Blitz until finely chopped, adding a little more oil if needed.

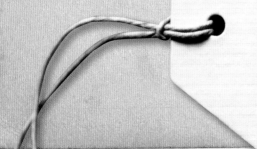

To freeze
Leave to cool. Pack into 2 plastic containers, seal and label. Freeze for up to 2 months.

To serve from frozen
Thaw at room temperature for 2 hours. Heat through in a covered saucepan. Add to cooked tagliatelle and sprinkle with freshly grated Parmesan, black pepper and basil leaves. Or microwave a 2 person portion in a covered dish for 5 minutes on full power in the microwave. Stir before serving.

MIXED BEAN PUTTANESCA SAUCE

SERVES 4

PREP: 15 MINUTES

COOK: 25 MINUTES

REHEAT FROM FROZEN: 7–8 MINUTES IN THE MICROWAVE OR 15 MINUTES IN A SAUCEPAN

Heat 1 tbsp olive oil in a saucepan, add 1 finely chopped onion and cook gently for 5 minutes. Add 115g/4oz cubed chorizo sausage and cook for 2–3 minutes, until just beginning to brown. Stir in 450g/1lb roughly chopped tomatoes (peel them first if you like) and ½ tsp smoked hot paprika. Cook for 1 minute, then mix in 1 tbsp tomato purée (tomato paste), 300ml/ ½ pint/1¼ cups vegetable stock, salt and pepper. Bring to the boil, then simmer, uncovered, for 10 minutes.

Add 250g/9oz shelled broad (fava) beans and 200g/7oz thinly sliced runner (string) beans to a large saucepan of boiling water, bring back to the boil, cook for 3 minutes, then drain and cool quickly in iced water. Drain again.

Stir the cooled green veggies into the sauce with 85g/3oz chopped olives and a handful of chopped parsley.

To freeze

Leave to cool. Pack into individual plastic containers, seal and label. Freeze for up to 2 months.

To serve from frozen

Transfer a portion to a dish, cover and microwave on full power for 7–8 minutes, stirring twice, until piping hot. Or reheat in a covered saucepan over a low heat for 15 minutes stirring until piping hot. Add to cooked pasta shells and sprinkle with freshly grated Parmesan.

ROASTED BUTTERNUT SQUASH AND PARSNIP SAUCE

SERVES 4

PREP: 15 MINUTES

COOK: 50 MINUTES

REHEAT FROM FROZEN: 5–6 MINUTES IN THE MICROWAVE
OR 15 MINUTES IN A SAUCEPAN

Preheat the oven to 190°C/375°F/Gas Mark 5. Peel, deseed and cube 450g/1lb butternut squash; peel and cube 450g/1lb parsnips; cut 2 onions into wedges. Put the vegetables in a roasting pan and drizzle with 2 tbsp olive oil and 2 tbsp runny honey; sprinkle with ½ tsp dried crushed chillies, 1 tsp fennel seeds, 3 finely chopped garlic cloves and plenty of salt and pepper. Roast for 45–55 minutes until the vegetables are beginning to caramelize around the edges. Add 450ml/16fl oz/2 cups vegetable stock and 2 tbsp sherry or balsamic vinegar and bring to the boil, stirring.

To serve, stir in 125ml/4fl oz/½ cup crème fraîche and mix with cooked pasta. Sprinkle with a few walnut pieces or freshly grated Parmesan.

To freeze
Leave to cool. Pack single portions into plastic bags, seal and label. Freeze for up to 2 months.

To serve from frozen
Transfer a portion to a dish, cover and microwave on full power for 5-6 minutes, stirring twice, until piping hot. Or reheat from frozen in a covered saucepan over a low heat for 15 minutes, stirring and increasing the heat as the sauce thaws. Finish with 2 tbsp crème fraîche per portion, add to cooked pasta and sprinkle with walnut pieces or grated Parmesan.

CHEESY MAC

SERVES 4

PREP: 15 MINUTES

COOK: 7–8 MINUTES

REHEAT FROM FROZEN: MICROWAVE 6–7 MINUTES OR
THAW OVERNIGHT AND 5 MINUTES IN A SAUCEPAN,
FINISH UNDER THE GRILL

Melt 55g/2oz/4 tbsp butter in a saucepan, stir in 55g/2oz/½ cup plain (all-purpose) flour and cook for 1 minute. Gradually mix in 600ml/1 pint/2½ cups milk and bring to the boil, stirring. Mix in 2 tsp Dijon mustard, 140g/5oz/1¼ cups grated Cheddar or Gruyère cheese, salt and pepper. Cook gently, stirring, for 2–3 minutes, until the sauce is smooth. Take off the heat.

Add 140g/5oz/generous 1 cup cubed carrots and the kernels cut from 1 corn cob to a saucepan of boiling water, bring back to the boil and cook for 2 minutes. Add 115g/4oz sliced green beans and cook for 2 minutes, then add 115g/4oz broccoli, cut into small florets, and cook for 1 minute. Drain, cool quickly and drain again, then stir into the cooled sauce.

To serve, cook 350g/12oz dried macaroni for 10 minutes. Gently reheat the sauce, stir in macaroni. Tip into a shallow ovenproof dish, sprinkle with a little extra grated cheese and a few frozen breadcrumbs, grill under a medium heat until golden.

To freeze
Pack into individual plastic containers, seal and label. Freeze for up to 2 months.

To serve from frozen
Transfer a portion to a dish, cover, microwave on full power for 6-7 minutes, stirring twice, until piping hot. Or thaw overnight in the fridge and reheat in a saucepan, stirring, for 5 minutes, adding a little extra milk if needed. Finish as above.

GOAT'S CHEESE AND ROASTED PEPPER TART

SERVES 4–6

PREP: 30 MINUTES
CHILL: 30 MINUTES
COOK: 45 MINUTES
COOK FROM FROZEN: 45–55 MINUTES

225g/8oz/1¾ CUPS PLAIN (ALL-PURPOSE) FLOUR,
    PLUS EXTRA FOR DUSTING
55g/2oz/4 TBSP BUTTER, CUBED, PLUS EXTRA
    FOR GREASING
55g/2oz/4 TBSP WHITE VEGETABLE FAT (VEGETABLE
    SHORTENING), CUBED

Filling

3 PEPPERS (1 RED, 1 YELLOW, 1 ORANGE OR GREEN),
    QUARTERED AND DESEEDED
1 TBSP OLIVE OIL
SALT AND FRESHLY GROUND BLACK PEPPER
4 TSP PESTO
4 TBSP FRESHLY GRATED PARMESAN CHEESE
100g/3½oz GOAT'S CHEESE, CUBED
LEAVES FROM 2–3 SPRIGS OF FRESH BASIL, ROUGHLY
    CHOPPED
8 OLIVES, PITTED (OPTIONAL)

Egg custard

3 EGGS
250ml/8fl oz/1 CUP MILK, OR HALF MILK AND
    HALF DOUBLE (HEAVY) CREAM

Frozen quiches and savoury tarts can sometimes taste a little watery when thawed. To avoid this, bake the pastry shell blind, then add the filling and freeze – but finish with the egg custard after you take the tart from the freezer and when ready to bake.

1. Butter a 24cm/9½in loose-bottomed fluted tart tin. Put the flour in a bowl or food processor with a pinch of salt, add the fats and rub in with your fingertips or pulse in the processor to fine crumbs. Gradually mix in about 3 tbsp cold water to make a smooth dough.

2. Knead lightly on a lightly floured surface, then roll out thinly until a little larger than the tin. Lift the pastry over the rolling pin and unroll into the tart tin. Press it over the bottom and up the sides, then trim the pastry just above the rim of the tin. Prick the bottom with a fork and chill for 30 minutes.

3. Preheat the oven to 190°C/375°F/Gas Mark 5. Put the tart tin on a baking sheet, line the pastry with baking parchment and baking beans and bake for 10 minutes. Remove the paper and beans and cook for another 5 minutes until the pastry is dry and crisp. Turn the oven down to 180°C/350°F/Gas Mark 4.

4. Meanwhile, make the filling. Put the peppers in a single layer on a foil-lined grill (broiler) pan with the skins uppermost, brush with the oil and sprinkle with salt and pepper. Grill for about 10 minutes, until the skins are charred and the peppers softened. Enclose in the foil and leave to cool.

Recipe continues…

GOAT'S CHEESE TART
...CONTINUED

5. Unwrap the peppers, peel away the skins, then slice the peppers. Spread pesto over the base of the tart, arrange the peppers on top, then sprinkle the cheeses and basil leaves over, plus the olives, if using.

6. Beat the eggs and milk, or milk and cream, with salt and pepper, pour into the pastry shell and bake in an oven reduced to 180°C/350°F/Gas Mark 4 for 30 minutes, until golden and set. Allow to cool for 10 minutes then serve.

To freeze
After step 5, wrap the tart, still in its tin, in clingfilm (plastic wrap). If preferred, take out of the tin once frozen, wrap and pack in a plastic container for added protection. Seal, label and freeze for up to 3 months.

To serve from frozen
Preheat the oven to 180°C/350°F/Gas Mark 4. Unwrap the tart and put back in the tin if needed. Beat the eggs and milk, or milk and cream, with salt and pepper, then pour into the pastry shell. Bake for 45–55 minutes, until the top is golden and the custard set. Cover with foil after 40 minutes if the top seems to be browning too quickly.

ALSO TRY THIS...
LEEK AND
GRUYÈRE TART

Make the tart case and bake blind as above. Spread 2 tsp Dijon mustard over the pastry. Heat 40g/1½oz/3 tbsp butter in a frying pan, add 350g/12oz thinly sliced leeks and the leaves from 2–3 sprigs of fresh thyme. Gently cook for 3–4 minutes, stirring until softened. Grate 115g/4oz Gruyère cheese, sprinkle half over the pastry, top with the leeks and then the remaining cheese. Freeze and complete with the egg custard as above.

MUSHROOM. SHALLOT AND WALNUT BOURGUIGNON

SERVES 4

PREP: 25 MINUTES

COOK: 1 HOUR 10 MINUTES

REHEAT FROM FROZEN: 1 HOUR

2 TBSP OLIVE OIL

450g/1lb (ABOUT 20 SMALL) SHALLOTS

25g/1oz/2 TBSP BUTTER

450g/1lb CHESTNUT (CREMINI) CUP MUSHROOMS, HALVED

250g/9oz (ABOUT 3 LARGE) PORTOBELLO MUSHROOMS, THICKLY SLICED

2–3 GARLIC CLOVES, FINELY CHOPPED

1 TBSP PLAIN (ALL-PURPOSE) FLOUR

175ml/6fl oz/¾ CUP RED WINE

250ml/8fl oz/1 CUP VEGETABLE STOCK

1 TBSP TOMATO PURÉE (TOMATO PASTE)

55g/2oz/SCANT ½ CUP WALNUT HALVES

SMALL BUNCH OF FRESH HERBS OR 1 BOUQUET GARNI

SALT AND FRESHLY GROUND BLACK PEPPER

This hearty winter casserole with a rich red wine sauce will win round even ardent meat eaters. There's no need to thaw, just reheat from frozen for an easy weekend supper.

1. Preheat the oven to 160°C/325°F/Gas Mark 3. Heat 1 tbsp of the oil in a large frying pan, add the shallots and cook for 5 minutes, stirring until golden brown. Using a slotted spoon, transfer to a casserole dish.

2. Add the remaining oil and the butter to the pan, add the mushrooms and cook for 3 minutes, until just beginning to brown. Add the garlic and cook for 2 minutes.

3. Sprinkle the flour over the mushrooms, then stir in the wine, stock, tomato purée and walnuts. Add the herbs and season with salt and pepper. Bring to the boil, stirring, then transfer to the casserole dish.

4. Cover and cook in the oven for 1 hour.

5. Serve in shallow soup plates, with hot celeriac mash.

CELERIAC (CELERY ROOT) MASH

Peel and roughly chop 1 medium trimmed celeriac (celery root) and 1 large baking potato. Cook both together in boiling water for 15–20 minutes until tender. Drain and mash with 25g/1oz/2 tbsp butter, 4–6 tbsp milk or double (heavy) cream, a little grated nutmeg and salt and pepper to taste.

To serve from frozen

Preheat the oven to 180°C/350°F/Gas Mark 4. Cook the frozen Bourguignon, with its lid on, for 1 hour until piping hot, stirring once during cooking and again at the end. Cook frozen celeriac mash in its covered dish for 45 minutes, on the oven shelf below until piping hot, stirring once during cooking and again at the end.

To freeze

At the end of step 4, leave the Bourguignon to cool completely. Pack into a 23cm/9in square, 5cm/2in deep foil dish. Add the lid, seal and label. Freeze for up to 3 months. Freeze celeriac mash (see above) in the same type of dish.

SMOKED AUBERGINE
TAGINE

Grilling the aubergines (eggplants) adds a wonderful smoky flavour to this dish. Grilling them over the dying embers of a barbecue would be perfect, and once cooked they can be stored in the fridge overnight to make this dish the next day. The aubergines can also be cooked directly over a low gas flame.

SERVES 4

PREP: 25 MINUTES

COOK: ABOUT 1 HOUR

REHEAT FROM FROZEN: 8–10 MINUTES IN THE MICROWAVE
OR 35–40 MINUTES IN THE OVEN

2 LARGE AUBERGINES (EGGPLANTS)
1 TBSP OLIVE OIL
1 ONION, ROUGHLY CHOPPED
2–3 GARLIC CLOVES, FINELY CHOPPED
4cm/1½in PIECE FRESH GINGER, PEELED AND
    FINELY CHOPPED
450g/1lb COURGETTES (ZUCCHINI), CUBED
1 TSP TURMERIC
2 TSP HARISSA PASTE
400g CAN CHOPPED TOMATOES
400g CAN CHICKPEAS, DRAINED AND RINSED
250ml/8fl oz/1 CUP VEGETABLE STOCK
SALT AND FRESHLY GROUND BLACK PEPPER

To finish

225g/8oz RUNNER (STRING) BEANS, THINLY SLICED
200g/7oz WHOLEWHEAT COUSCOUS
1 TBSP OLIVE OIL
GRATED ZEST AND JUICE OF 1 UNWAXED LEMON
450ml/16fl oz/2 CUPS BOILING WATER
SMALL HANDFUL OF FRESH MINT, CHOPPED

1. Prick each aubergine two or three times. Grill (broil) about 5cm/2in away from a medium heat for 10–15 minutes, turning several times, until the skin is charred and the flesh soft.

2. Leave to cool slightly, then peel off the skin and roughly chop the flesh.

3. Heat the oil in a saucepan, add the onion and cook for 5 minutes, until just beginning to turn golden. Add the garlic, ginger, courgettes, turmeric and harissa and cook for 1 minute.

4. Add the tomatoes, chickpeas, stock and aubergine flesh. Season with salt and pepper and bring to the boil, stirring. Cover and simmer gently for 45 minutes, stirring from time to time.

5. When the tagine is almost ready, cook the green beans in boiling water for 5 minutes, until just tender, then drain.

6. Put the couscous in a bowl, add the oil, lemon zest and juice and a little salt and pepper, pour the boiling water over then cover and leave to stand for 5 minutes. Add the mint and fluff up the couscous with a fork.

7. Spoon the couscous into shallow bowls, top with the tagine and beans and sprinkle with extra mint.

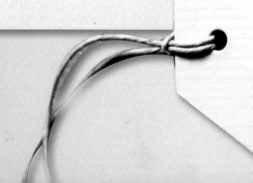

To freeze
At the end of step 6, spoon couscous in a ring around the edges of 4 microwavable or ovenproof dishes, spoon the tagine in the centre and top with the beans. Cover and leave to cool. Seal, label and freeze for up to 3 months.

To serve from frozen
Loosen the lid and microwave one portion at a time for 8-10 minutes on full power, stirring twice. Leave to stand for 2 minutes before serving. Or reheat in a preheated oven at 180°C/350°F/Gas Mark 4 for 35-40 minutes, stirring twice until piping hot.

POTATO DAUPHINOISE

Wonderfully creamy and indulgent, this version of the French classic has a thyme and garlicky scented layer of sautéed leek in the centre. Bake from frozen and enjoy with a crisp green salad speckled with crunchy pieces of walnut or as an accompaniment to grilled steak or lamb chops.

SERVES 4–6
PREP: 15 MINUTES
COOK: 40 MINUTES
COOK FROM FROZEN: 45–55 MINUTES

1.25kg/2lb 12oz POTATOES, PEELED AND VERY THINLY SLICED
4 TSP OLIVE OIL
1 SMALL LEEK, THINLY SLICED
3 GARLIC CLOVES, FINELY CHOPPED
LEAVES FROM 2–3 SPRIGS OF FRESH THYME
SALT AND FRESHLY GROUND BLACK PEPPER
2 TSP CORNFLOUR (CORNSTARCH) (SEE COOK'S TIPS)
450ml/16fl oz/2 CUPS DOUBLE (HEAVY) CREAM
15g/½ oz/1 TBSP BUTTER, DICED

1. Bring a large saucepan of water to the boil, add the potatoes and simmer for 3–5 minutes, until almost cooked. Timing will depend on how thinly you cut the potatoes, so check after 3 minutes and cook a little longer if needed. Drain in a colander.

2. Use a little of the oil to brush a 23cm/9in square, 5cm/2in deep foil dish. Heat the remaining oil in a small frying pan, then add the leek, garlic and thyme and cook gently for 4–5 minutes, until softened.

3. Spoon half the potatoes into the foil dish, spread evenly, and sprinkle with salt and pepper. Spoon the leek mixture over the top, then cover with the remaining potatoes and sprinkle with salt and pepper.

4. Mix the cornflour, if using, with a little of the cream until smooth, then stir in the remaining cream. Pour over the potatoes and dot the top with the butter.

5. To serve, bake in an oven preheated to 180°C/350°F/Gas Mark 4, for 30 minutes, until golden.

To serve from frozen

Preheat the oven to 180°C/350°F/Gas Mark 4. Remove the lid and cook for 45-55 minutes until the potatoes are piping hot and golden brown. Check after 30 minutes and loosely cover with the lid if they seem to be browning too quickly.

COOK'S TIPS

• If you plan to serve this dish without freezing, omit the cornflour (cornstarch) – this just helps to stabilize the sauce when it is cooked from frozen.
• If you like, crumble a little blue cheese and sprinkle over the leeks.
• Add a few chopped anchovies to the leeks and a few more, cut into strips, on top before baking.

To freeze
At the end of step 4, leave to cool completely. Cover with the lid, seal and label. Freeze for up to 2 months.

EMERGENCY SNACKS

For a quick lunch or after-school snack, delve into the freezer for one of these cheesy treats.

CHEESE AND CHUTNEY TOASTIES

SERVES 4
PREP: 10 MINUTES
REHEAT FROM FROZEN: 8 MINUTES

Spread 8 slices of bread thinly with butter taken from 75g/2½oz/5 tbsp butter at room temperature. Spread 4–6 tsp mango or tomato chutney over half the bread, then sprinkle with 2 finely chopped spring onions (scallions) and 140g/5oz/1¼ cups grated Cheddar cheese. Cover with the remaining bread, then spread the remaining butter thinly over the outside of each sandwich.

To serve, heat a non-stick frying pan over a low to medium heat. Cook the sandwiches for about 4 minutes, turning several times and pressing down with a spatula until golden on both sides. Cut into quarters and serve with tomato wedges.

To freeze
Wrap each sandwich in clingfilm before the serving instructions. Freeze for up to 2 months.

To serve from frozen
Unwrap. Cook as above for 8 minutes.

CAULIFLOWER WELSH RAREBIT

SERVES 4
PREP: 15 MINUTES
COOK: 8 MINUTES
COOK FROM FROZEN: 5–6 MINUTES IN THE MICROWAVE OR 30–35 MINUTES IN THE OVEN AND 3 MINUTES GRILLING

Cut 2 medium cauliflowers into florets and steam over boiling water for 8 minutes until just tender. Meanwhile, melt 55g/2oz/4 tbsp butter in a saucepan, stir in 4 finely chopped spring onions (scallions) and cook gently for 2 minutes until softened. Stir in 55g/2oz/½ cup plain (all-purpose) flour, then gradually mix in 450ml/16fl oz/2 cups milk. Bring to the boil, stirring until thickened and smooth. Mix in 2 tsp wholegrain or Dijon mustard, 2 tsp Worcestershire sauce (not suitable for vegetarians), 4 tbsp lager or blonde beer or extra milk and 140g/5oz/1¼ cups grated Cheddar cheese until the cheese has melted.

Divide cauliflower between 4 freezer containers – ovenproof china or foil. Pour sauce over the cauliflower, sprinkle with 25g/1oz/3 tbsp grated Cheddar cheese and 2 tbsp breadcrumbs.

To serve now, cook under a medium grill until piping hot and golden brown.

To freeze
Leave to cool before the grilling stage. Cover, seal and label. Freeze for up to 2 months.

To serve from frozen
Microwave in ovenproof china dish for 5–6 minutes on full power, stirring twice one dish at a time, then brown under a medium grill. Or cook from frozen uncovered in a foil dish for 30–35 minutes, until piping hot and golden brown and grill for 3 minutes.

CHEESY JACKETS

SERVES 4
PREP: 15 MINUTES
COOK: 45–60 MINUTES
REHEAT FROM FROZEN: 25–30 MINUTES IN THE OVEN

Preheat the oven to 200°C/400°F/Gas Mark 6.
Scrub and prick 4 x 200g/7oz baking potatoes
with a fork, then rub 1 tbsp sunflower oil over them.
Bake for 45–60 minutes, until the skins are crisp
and the centres soft.

Cut the potatoes in half lengthwise, scoop out the
centres and mash in a bowl. Lightly beat 2 eggs
and stir into the mash with 115g/4oz/1 cup grated
Cheddar or Gruyère cheese, 2 finely chopped
spring onions (scallions) and 4 tomatoes, cut into
wedges, deseeded and chopped. Leave to cool,
then mix in 115g/4oz/scant 1 cup sweetcorn
(cooked if serving now, frozen if going straight into
the freezer). Spoon into the skins and sprinkle with
40g/1½oz/6 tbsp grated cheese.

To serve now, grill the potatoes under a medium
heat while still hot for 5 minutes or bake from cold
at 200°C/400°F/Gas Mark 6 for 15 minutes.

To freeze
Pack 2 potato halves in each of 4 foil freezer
containers, cover, seal and label. Freeze for up
to 2 months.

To serve from frozen
Preheat the oven to 200°C/400°F/Gas Mark
6. Remove lids and cook potatoes for 25–
30 minutes until piping hot and golden brown.

MUSHROOM AND PESTO PUFF TARTS

MAKES 6
PREP: 15 MINUTES
COOK: 18 MINUTES
COOK FROM FROZEN: 18–20 MINUTES

Preheat the oven to 200°C/400°F/Gas Mark
6. Unroll a 310g/11oz roll of chilled puff pastry,
cut a thin sliver from each edge, then cut into
6 squares. Put each square on a large foil-lined
baking sheet. Using a fork, prick the centre of each
pastry square about 2cm/¾in from the edge.
Spread 1 tbsp pesto over the centres.

Mix 140g/5oz quartered closed-cup mushrooms
with 140g/5oz halved cherry tomatoes, 1 tbsp
olive oil and 140g/5oz cubed mozzarella, season
and spoon over the pastry squares.

If not freezing, bake for 12–15 minutes, until well
risen around the edges and pale golden.

To freeze
Open-freeze raw tarts on a baking sheet until
hard then individually wrap in clingfilm or foil,
seal and label. Freeze for up to 2 months.

To serve from frozen
Preheat the oven to 180°C/350°F/Gas Mark 4.
Put the frozen unwrapped tarts on a baking
sheet, bake for 10 minutes, loosely cover with foil
and cook 10 minutes more.

BREAD

BREAD

What could be nicer than the smell of homemade bread wafting through the house – and no clearing up to do? Make a large batch of bread when you are in the mood for cooking or have young children in need of a rainy day activity. Freeze your yeasty goodies either cooked or shaped and ready to rise overnight, then leave to thaw before baking in the morning.

Making bread is simple if you use easy-blend dried (active dry) yeast. This can be kept in the cupboard for months (check the best before date). Just add it to strong bread flour with a little salt and sugar, some butter or oil to prevent the dough from becoming stale too quickly, and warm water or milk to activate it. Knead well, then shape and leave to rise. The longer you knead and pummel the dough for, the more you'll develop the gluten and the better the bread will be. Don't confuse easy-blend yeast with traditional dried yeast, which must be frothed with warm liquid before use. Check the packet.

Yeast needs warmth to grow. Warm water from the tap or milk gently heated in a small saucepan should feel just warm to your little finger, or 37°C/98.4°F on a cook's thermometer. Too hot and the yeast will be killed, so err on the side of caution, then leave the dough in a warm kitchen to do its stuff.

The freezer life of bread depends on how crisp and crusty it is and how rich the dough is: the more butter, milk or eggs, the less time it will keep for in the freezer. During freezing the crust on very crusty bread tends to crack and break, so softer, floury finishes are best.

If you keep a sliced loaf in the freezer, you can take out a slice and pop it in the toaster while still frozen. You can also freeze prepared sandwiches such as ham, chicken, canned tuna, smoked salmon or smoked mackerel mixed with a little full-fat cream cheese or grated cheese. Flavour with mustard or chutney rather than mayonnaise. Don't include tomatoes, cucumber or salad leaves, as they go soggy when thawed.

PIZZA

Kids love to help make their own pizza, so why not make enough for two meals, eat half now and freeze the others for another night? You might also like to do a simple Margherita pizza, with tomato sauce, sliced mozzarella and a few extra basil leaves, for younger children.

MAKES 8

PREP: 55 MINUTES, PLUS 30 MINUTES RISING

COOK: 10 MINUTES

COOK FROM FROZEN: 15–20 MINUTES

500g/1lb 2oz/4 CUPS STRONG WHITE BREAD FLOUR,
   PLUS EXTRA FOR DUSTING
1 TSP SALT
1 TSP CASTER (SUPERFINE) SUGAR
2 TSP EASY-BLEND DRIED (ACTIVE DRY) YEAST
4 TBSP OLIVE OIL

Tomato sauce

1 TBSP OLIVE OIL
1 ONION, FINELY CHOPPED
2 X 400G CANS CHOPPED TOMATOES
1 TBSP CASTER (SUPERFINE) SUGAR
1 TBSP TOMATO PUREE (TOMATO PASTE)
HANDFUL OF FRESH BASIL, ROUGHLY TORN
SALT AND FRESHLY GROUND BLACK PEPPER

Toppings

SEE PAGE 100

1. First make the tomato sauce. Heat the oil in a saucepan, add the onion and cook for 5 minutes, stirring from time to time, until just beginning to colour. Add the tomatoes, sugar, tomato purée, basil, salt and pepper and cook, uncovered, for 10 minutes, stirring from time to time and breaking up the tomatoes, until the sauce has thickened. Set aside to cool.

2. To make the pizza bases, put the flour, salt, sugar and yeast in a large bowl and stir. Add the oil, then gradually mix in 250–300ml/8–10fl oz/1–1¼ cups warm water (see page 96) to make a soft dough. Turn out onto a lightly floured surface and knead for at least 5 minutes, until the dough is smooth and elastic.

3. Cut the dough into 8 pieces, then roll out each piece thinly to a rough 20cm/8in diameter round. If cooking now, put the dough on to an oiled baking sheet. To freeze, put the dough on to a piece of baking parchment.

4. Spread the tops with the cooled tomato sauce, then add your chosen toppings. Loosely cover the pizzas with oiled clingfilm and leave in a warm place for 30 minutes for the bases to rise.

5. If not freezing: preheat the oven to 220°F/425°F/Gas Mark 7. Cook the pizzas for 10 minutes, until golden.

Recipe continues..

PIZZA
...CONTINUED

To serve from frozen

Preheat the oven to 190°C/375°F/Gas Mark 5. Remove the clingfilm and put as many pizzas as you need onto baking sheets. Bake for 15–20 minutes, until golden, piping hot and the base is crisp.

Toppings, each for 2 pizzas

Antipasta

200g/7oz CHILLED ANTIPASTA IN OLIVE OIL (GRIDDLED ARTICHOKE HEARTS, SLICED MUSHROOMS, SUNBLUSH TOMATOES, STONED OLIVES)
140g/5oz MOZZARELLA, THINLY SLICED
A FEW FRESH BASIL LEAVES

Three-cheese

140g/5oz MOZZARELLA, THINLY SLICED
55g/2oz ROQUEFORT CHEESE, CUBED
SHAVINGS OF PARMESAN CHEESE
A FEW BLACK OLIVES, STONED

Pesto and mushroom

4 TSP OLIVE OIL
200g/7oz BUTTON MUSHROOMS OR MIXED MUSHROOMS, SLICED
140g/5oz MOZZARELLA, THINLY SLICED
4 TSP PESTO

Spinach and chorizo

85g/3oz SPINACH, RINSED, DRAINED AND COOKED FOR 2–3 MINUTES IN A DRY PAN UNTIL JUST WILTED
55g/2oz CHORIZO, CUBED
140g/5oz MOZZARELLA, THINLY SLICED

To freeze

At the end of step 4, open-freeze the pizzas, still loosely covered with clingfilm, until firm. Wrap completely in clingfilm, seal and label. Freeze for up to 2 months.

FARMHOUSE WHITE BREAD

MAKES 2 X 900g/2lb LOAVES

PREP: 25 MINUTES

RISING: ABOUT 1½ HOURS

COOK: 25–30 MINUTES

COOK FROM FROZEN: THAW UNCOOKED DOUGH OVERNIGHT THEN COOK FOR 25–30 MINUTES; THAW COOKED LOAF FOR 2–3 HOURS

SUNFLOWER OIL, FOR GREASING

1kg/2lb 4oz/8 CUPS STRONG WHITE BREAD FLOUR, PLUS EXTRA FOR DUSTING

55g/2oz/4 TBSP BUTTER, CUBED

2 TBSP CASTER (SUPERFINE) SUGAR

2 TSP SALT

2½ TSP EASY-BLEND DRIED (ACTIVE DRY) YEAST

Nothing beats the wonderful aroma of bread baking in the oven. So why not make two loaves: one to eat now and one to freeze? Easy-blend dried (active dry) yeast can be simply stirred into the flour without the need to froth it first in warm water. The bread can be frozen raw or cooked.

1. Brush 2 x 900g/2lb loaf tins lightly but evenly with sunflower oil

2. Put the flour and butter in a large bowl and rub the butter into the flour until it resembles fine crumbs. Stir in the sugar, salt and yeast, then gradually mix in 600ml/1 pint/2½ cups warm water (see page 96) to make a soft dough – you may need to add up to another 150ml/5fl oz/⅔ cup warm water.

3. Turn out onto a lightly floured surface and knead the dough for 5 minutes, until smooth and elastic. Dust the bowl with a little flour, return the dough to the bowl, cover the top loosely with oiled clingfilm and leave in a warm place to rise for 45–60 minutes.

4. Knock the dough back with your fist, then turn it out on to a work surface and knead again. Divide in half, shape each half to the length of the loaf tin, then press into the tins and cover the tops loosely with oiled clingfilm. Leave to rise for 30–40 minutes, until the dough is just above the top of the tin.

5. Preheat the oven to 220°C/425°F/Gas Mark 7. Remove the clingfilm, dust the loaves with flour and cook for 25 minutes, until golden brown and the bread sounds hollow when tapped. Turn out onto a wire rack and serve warm or cold.

To serve from frozen

If you freeze partly risen dough in step 4, loosen the clingfilm and thaw in the fridge overnight or for up to 2 hours, then for 45-60 minutes at room temperature. Preheat the oven to 220°C/425°F/Gas Mark 7. Remove the clingfilm, lightly dust the loaf with flour and bake for 25-30 minutes.

Thaw a cooked wrapped loaf for 2-3 hours at room temperature.

To freeze

Allow to rise for just 20 minutes in step 4. Overwrap with a second layer of clingfilm. Seal and freeze for up to 2 months. Or freeze baked, cooled bread wrapped in clingfilm for up to 4 months.

GLUTEN-FREE WALNUT BREAD

Gluten-free bread can be expensive to buy and goes stale quickly, so making and freezing your own is a tasty alternative. Unlike bread made with wheat flour, gluten-free flours are mixed to form a thick batter and work best baked in loaf tins.

MAKES 2 X 450g/1lb LOAVES
PREP: 15 MINUTES, PLUS 45–60 MINUTES RISING
COOK: 30–40 MINUTES, OR 20 MINUTES FOR A MINI LOAF
SERVE FROM FROZEN: THAW 2–3 HOURS, REHEAT
    20 MINUTES IN THE OVEN

SUNFLOWER OIL, FOR GREASING
450g/1lb/SCANT 4 CUPS GLUTEN-FREE BREAD FLOUR
1 TSP SALT
2 TBSP LIGHT BROWN SUGAR
2 TSP EASY-BLEND DRIED (ACTIVE DRY) YEAST
1 TSP MALT OR WHITE WINE VINEGAR
6 TBSP OLIVE OIL
2 EGGS
85g/3oz/SCANT ¾ CUP WALNUT PIECES
2 TBSP SUNFLOWER SEEDS

1. Lightly brush 2 x 450g/1lb loaf tins with oil.

2. Put the flour, salt, sugar and yeast in a large mixing bowl. In a separate bowl, lightly beat together the vinegar, oil and eggs, then stir them into the dry ingredients and gradually mix in about 325ml/11fl oz/scant 1½ cups warm water (see page 96) to make a smooth, thick batter.

3. Stir in the walnut pieces, then divide the bread mixture between the prepared tins. Sprinkle with the sunflower seeds, then loosely cover the tops of the tins with lightly oiled clingfilm and leave in a warm place for 45–60 minutes, until the bread is well risen and just above the top of the tins.

4. Preheat the oven to 220°C/425°F/Gas Mark 7. Remove the clingfilm, put the tins on a baking sheet and bake for 30–40 minutes, until well risen, golden brown and the bread sounds hollow when gently tapped. Loosen the edges of the bread, turn out on to a wire rack and leave to cool. Serve warm or cold.

ALSO TRY
• For herb bread, stir in a handful of finely chopped mixed fresh herbs instead of the walnuts.
• For apricot and cranberry bread, stir in a few chopped ready-to-eat (plumped) dried apricots and some dried cranberries instead of the walnuts.

To serve from frozen
Thaw the loaves at room temperature for 2-3 hours, then warm through in a low oven, or reaheat a foil-wrapped loaf in an oven preheated to 180°C/350°F/Gas Mark 4 for 20 minutes.

To freeze
Cool the cooked loaf completely, then wrap loaves individually in clingfilm (plastic wrap), seal and label. If you plan to serve the bread as toast you may prefer to slice the larger loaf and then pack in a resealable plastic bag. Toast from frozen. Freeze for up to 2 months.

CORIANDER AND CUMIN NAAN BREADS

MAKES 8

PREP: 30 MINUTES, PLUS 1–1¼ HOURS RISING

COOK: 8–10 MINUTES

COOK FROM FROZEN: THAW UNCOOKED DOUGH FOR 1¼ HOURS AT ROOM TEMPERATURE, THEN COOK FOR 10 MINUTES; REHEAT COOKED BREADS FOR 10 MINUTES

500g/1lb·2oz/4 CUPS STRONG WHITE BREAD FLOUR, PLUS EXTRA FOR DUSTING

HANDFUL OF FRESH CORIANDER (CILANTRO), ROUGHLY CHOPPED

SALT AND FRESHLY GROUND BLACK PEPPER

1 TSP CUMIN SEEDS

1 TSP CASTER (SUPERFINE) SUGAR

2 TSP EASY-BLEND DRIED (ACTIVE DRY) YEAST

55g/2oz/4 TBSP BUTTER OR GHEE, MELTED

4 TBSP LOW-FAT NATURAL YOGURT

You don't need a special tandoor oven to make these, just bake under the grill or on a hot griddle pan until puffed and browned. They can be frozen raw or baked. A great accompaniment to curries or spiced barbecued meats.

1. Put the flour, coriander and cumin in a large mixing bowl, then season with pepper and stir in the sugar, yeast and 1 tsp salt.

2. Add the melted butter or ghee and yogurt, then gradually mix in 200–250ml/7–8fl oz/about 1 cup warm water (see page 96) to form a soft dough.

3. Turn the dough out on to a lightly floured surface and knead for 5 minutes, until smooth and elastic. Lightly dust the bowl with flour, add the dough, then cover the top loosely with oiled clingfilm and leave in a warm place for 45–60 minutes, or until doubled in size.

4. Knock the dough back with your fist, then turn out and knead well. Cut the dough into 8 pieces, then roll out each piece to a rough oval about 18cm/7in long. Place on 2 baking sheets lined with oiled clingfilm and leave to rise for 10–15 minutes, covered loosely with more oiled clingfilm, until puffy.

5. To serve, remove the clingfilm and cook under a hot grill or on a hot, ungreased griddle pan for 3–5 minutes on each side, until puffed and golden brown.

ALSO TRY

Replace the coriander and cumin with 1 tsp each of black mustard seeds and crushed black peppercorns or with finely crushed garlic and dried crushed chilli.

To serve from frozen

Loosen the wrappings on uncooked naan breads and leave to rise at room temperature for 1-1¼ hours. Unwrap and bake under a hot grill or on a hot, ungreased griddle pan for about 5 minutes on each side.

For baked naan breads, preheat the oven to 160°C/325°F/Gas Mark 3. Wrap in foil and bake from frozen in a single layer for 10 minutes, or until hot.

To freeze

At the end of step 4, freeze the breads on the baking sheets, uncovered, for 2-3 hours. Peel off the clingfilm and wrap loaves individually in lightly oiled clingfilm, then pack in a plastic container and seal. To freeze after cooking, leave to cool. Wrap individually in foil and pack in a plastic container. Freeze for up to 2 months.

RUSTIC APPLE
CHEESE AND MUSTARD
SCONES

These do not contain yeast and can be made and baked in less than 45 minutes. Delicious served warm with a bowl of lettuce and garden herb soup (see page 70) or with cold meats and pickles for lunch.

MAKES 2 LOAVES OR 12 WEDGES
PREP: 25 MINUTES
COOK: 20 MINUTES
REHEAT FROM FROZEN: 15–35 MINUTES

SUNFLOWER OIL, FOR GREASING
1 MEDIUM COOKING APPLE, CORED, PEELED AND CUBED
2 TBSP CIDER OR WHITE WINE VINEGAR
1 TBSP LIGHT BROWN SUGAR
1 TBSP WHOLEGRAIN MUSTARD
450g/1lb/SCANT 4 CUPS SELF-RAISING FLOUR, PLUS
   EXTRA FOR DUSTING
55g/2oz/4 TBSP BUTTER, CUBED
SALT AND FRESHLY GROUND BLACK PEPPER
175g/6oz MATURE CHEDDAR CHEESE, GRATED
2 EGGS, BEATEN
APPROX 90ml/6 TBSP MILK

1. Preheat the oven to 200°C/400°F/Gas Mark 6. Lightly oil a large baking sheet. Cook the apple in the vinegar, sugar and mustard in a small saucepan over a medium heat for 5 minutes, stirring from to time, until the apple is soft.

2. Put the flour, butter and seasoning in a mixing bowl and rub the butter into the flour until it resembles fine crumbs. Stir in the apple mixture and two-thirds of the cheese. Add three-quarters of the beaten egg, then gradually mix in enough milk for a soft dough.

3. Turn the dough out onto a lightly floured surface and knead briefly, until just smooth. Cut in half, then roll out each half to a circle about 2cm/¾in thick.

4. Transfer both dough rounds to the baking sheet, then cut each one into 6 wedges and separate them slightly to allow space for rising in the oven. Brush the tops with the remaining egg and sprinkle with the remaining cheese. Bake for 20 minutes, until golden brown and well risen. Serve warm from the oven.

ALSO TRY
Instead of the apple, vinegar and sugar mixture, add a few very finely chopped spring onions (scallions) or snipped chives with 1 tbsp wholegrain mustard.

To serve from frozen
Preheat the oven to 180°C/350°F/Gas Mark 4. Reheat from frozen while still wrapped in foil: 30–35 minutes for the whole scone-loaf, or 15–20 minutes for individually wrapped wedges, until piping hot.

To freeze
Place on a wire rack to cool completely. Either wrap the whole scone-loaf in foil, or separate the wedges and wrap individually. Seal, label and freeze for up to 2 months.

PARSLEY AND POTATO
FARLS

Indulge in a leisurely Sunday brunch and serve these soft potato scones warm with grilled bacon and scrambled eggs, or with cream cheese, smoked salmon and lemon wedges.

MAKES 16
PREP: 1 HOUR
COOK: 12–15 MINUTES
REHEAT FROM FROZEN: 15–20 MINUTES

SUNFLOWER OIL, FOR GREASING
350g/12oz POTATOES, PEELED AND ROUGHLY CHOPPED
250g/9oz/2 CUPS PLAIN (ALL-PURPOSE) FLOUR,
    PLUS EXTRA FOR DUSTING
1 TSP BICARBONATE OF SODA (BAKING SODA)
SALT
PINCH OF CAYENNE PEPPER
HANDFUL OF FRESH PARSLEY, ROUGHLY CHOPPED
140g/5oz/⅔ CUP LOW-FAT NATURAL YOGURT
1 EGG, BEATEN
1–2 TBSP MILK

1. Preheat the oven to 220°C/425°F/Gas Mark 7. Lightly brush a baking sheet with oil. Cook the potatoes in boiling water for 15 minutes, until tender. Drain, then mash and leave to cool for 10 minutes.

2. Sift the flour and bicarbonate of soda into the mashed potato, season with salt and cayenne pepper and mix with a fork. Add the parsley, yogurt and egg and fork together to make a smooth, soft dough, adding the milk if necessary.

3. Tip the dough on to a lightly floured surface, knead a little, then roll out to 2cm/¾in thick. Using a 5.5cm/2¼in round plain cutter, cut out circles and place on the baking sheet. Reroll the dough and cut out more circles until you have used all the dough.

4. Lightly dust the top of the farls with a little flour, then bake for 12–15 minutes, until well risen and golden brown.

5. Serve warm from the oven, split and buttered.

To serve from frozen
Preheat the oven to 180°C/350°F/Gas Mark 4. Take out as many frozen farls as you need, loosely wrap in foil and reheat for 15-20 minutes, until piping hot.

To freeze
At the end of step 4, cool on a wire rack. Pack in a plastic bag, seal and label. Freeze for up to 2 months.

FRUITED BABY BRIOCHE

Brioche is a wonderfully butter-rich yeasty bread. Freeze it raw and then bake when needed for a relaxed weekend breakfast. These little buns are stuffed with a mixture of prunes and dried sour cherries; you could also try sultanas and cranberries flavoured with grated orange zest, or a little grated marzipan and mixed dried fruit – chocoholics might like to add a square of chocolate.

MAKES 12

PREP: 45 MINUTES, PLUS 2–2½ HOURS RISING

COOK: 10–12 MINUTES

COOK FROM FROZEN: THAW UNCOOKED BRIOCHE
    OVERNIGHT, THEN COOK FOR 12–15 MINUTES; THAW
    COOKED BRIOCHE FOR 2 HOURS

350g/12oz/SCANT 3 CUPS STRONG WHITE BREAD FLOUR,
    PLUS EXTRA FOR DUSTING
½ TSP SALT
4 TBSP CASTER (SUPERFINE) SUGAR
2 TSP EASY-BLEND DRIED (ACTIVE DRY) YEAST
2 EGGS
1 TSP VANILLA EXTRACT
150ml/5fl oz/⅔ CUP WARM MILK
115g/4oz/½ CUP BUTTER, AT ROOM
    TEMPERATURE, CUBED
70g/2½oz READY-TO-EAT PITTED PRUNES,
    ROUGHLY CHOPPED
55g/2oz DRIED SOUR CHERRIES
BEATEN EGG, TO GLAZE
SIFTED ICING (CONFECTIONERS') SUGAR OR GLACÉ ICING,
    TO SERVE

1. Put the flour, salt, sugar and yeast in a large warmed bowl and stir together. Lightly beat the eggs, vanilla and warm milk together in a jug, then gradually mix into the dry ingredients to make a smooth, soft dough.

2. Knead for 5 minutes on a lightly floured surface, then put back in the bowl, cover with a clean cloth and leave to rise in a warm place for about 1½ hours, or until doubled in size.

3. Knock the dough back and knead it briefly. Gradually work in the butter, a few pieces at a time, resisting the temptation to mix in more flour. As more and more butter is added, the dough will become soft and sticky, so you may prefer to mix in a bowl with an electric beater or in a food processor fitted with a plastic blade. Once all the butter is added, the dough will be more like a batter. Leave to rest for 10 minutes. Lightly brush 12 brioche moulds or the cups of a muffin tin with butter or oil.

4. Divide the dough into 12 pieces. Add a few pieces of chopped prunes and dried cherries to the centre of each brioche, then shape into a ball and put into the buttered or oiled moulds. Cover lightly with oiled clingfilm and leave to rise for 30–40 minutes.

5. If not freezing, preheat the oven to 200°C/400°F/Gas Mark 6. Brush the tops of the brioches with beaten egg and bake for 10–12 minutes, until golden brown and the tops sound hollow when tapped. Leave to cool for a few minutes, then take out of the tins and dust with sifted icing sugar or a drizzle of glacé icing.

To serve from frozen

For partially risen dough, thaw overnight in the fridge, loosely covered with oiled clingfilm. Preheat the oven to 200°F/400°F/Gas Mark 6. Remove the clingfilm; the brioche should now be above the tins. Brush the tops with beaten egg, then bake for 12-15 minutes, until golden brown and the tops sound hollow when tapped. Leave to cool for a few minutes, then take out of the tins and dust with sifted icing sugar or a drizzle of glacé icing.

For cooked brioche, thaw at room temperature for 2 hours and then warm in a low oven.

COOK'S TIPS

A rich, sweet dough takes longer to rise than a plain one, so leave in a warm place to encourage rising. If your kitchen is very cold, stand the bowl over a saucepan of just-boiled water, or in the warming drawer under the cooker if you have one.

To freeze

In step 4, leave the brioche to rise for just 15-20 minutes. Open-freeze, still loosely covered with clingfilm, until firm. Wrap completely in clingfilm, seal and label. Freeze for up to 2 months.

Freeze cooked and cooled but undusted/drizzled brioche individually wrapped in foil.

FRUIT

FRUIT

Capture the flavour of raspberries, strawberries or juicy peaches when the season is at its height. There is something satisfying about having a luscious pudding ready for a gathering of family or friends. On a hot day, choose strawberry and Champagne jellies or raspberry cheesecake. For something more warming, try cherry crêpes. Whatever the occasion, your freezer can help you to make the most of fruit all year round.

Avoid washing berries and currants unless it is essential, as this will make them soft when they thaw. For redcurrants and blackcurrants, freeze a few on their stalks as a decoration; the rest should be destalked and open-frozen (see below) or puréed. Strawberries have a high water content, and as the water turns to ice it expands and breaks down the cell structure, so when the fruit thaws it collapses. Although their flavour isn't affected, they shouldn't be served whole. Instead, lightly cook them with a little water and sugar, or with lemon or elderflower cordial, to serve with ice-cream, or mix with other fruit for a pie or crumble, or fold them through whipped cream with crushed meringue.

Purée and sieve cooked strawberries, mixed berries or apples and blackberries, mix with a little lemon juice and icing sugar, and freeze in an ice-cube tray. Pop the frozen cubes into a plastic bag; they're great defrosted and served over ice-cream or stirred through natural yogurt.

Firmer orchard fruits such as apples and pears are best cooked before freezing, as they tend to discolour. Core, peel and dice or slice them and cook gently with a little water, lemon juice and sugar, or make a French-style tarte tatin or apple Betty.

Berries and cherries, blackberries and halved and stoned peaches, plums and apricots can be quickly open-frozen on a baking sheet; choose one with sides so the fruit doesn't roll off. Freeze for 2–3 hours, until hard, then pack in plastic boxes, cover, seal and label. Freezing this way will prevent the fruit from clumping together in the freezer.

Mixed berry Eton mess, see page 134.

STRAWBERRY CHAMPAGNE JELLIES

SERVES 8
PREP: 20 MINUTES, PLUS 3–4 HOURS SETTING
COOK: 6–7 MINUTES
SERVE FROM FROZEN: THAW 2–3 HOURS

3 TSP POWDERED GELATINE
680g/1½lb STRAWBERRIES, HULLED AND ROUGHLY
    CHOPPED
55g/2oz/4 TBSP CASTER (SUPERFINE) SUGAR
125ml/4fl oz/½ CUP DRY SPARKLING WHITE WINE
JUICE OF 1 LEMON
A FEW TINY STRAWBERRIES OR VIOLA FLOWERS,
    TO DECORATE
SINGLE (LIGHT) CREAM, TO SERVE

To serve from frozen

Thaw in the fridge overnight or at room temperature for 2–3 hours. To turn out from a silicone mould, loosen the edges, then invert on to a small plate, shake the mould and plate and then remove the mould. Dip metal moulds into a bowl of just-boiled water, count to three and then turn out.

You don't have to use Champagne for these fruity jellies: less expensive sparkling white wine works brilliantly and this is a good way to use up half a glass that may be left in the bottle – it doesn't matter if it is a little flat.

1. Pour 4 tbsp cold water into a small bowl and sprinkle the gelatine over the top. Stir and make sure the powder is absorbed by the water. Set aside for 5 minutes.

2. Put two-thirds of the strawberries in a saucepan with the sugar, sparkling wine and lemon juice. Cook gently for 5 minutes, until the strawberries have softened and the sugar has dissolved. Pour into a blender or food processor and whiz until smooth, then press through a sieve back into the pan.

3. Scoop the gelatine into the pan and heat gently, stirring constantly for 1–2 minutes, until it has dissolved. Take off the heat and leave to cool.

4. Stir the remaining strawberries into the jelly. Pour into 8 x 125ml/4fl oz/½ cup silicone or metal pudding moulds set on a small tray.

5. If not freezing, chill the puddings in the fridge for 3–4 hours, until set. Turn out, decorate with tiny strawberries or viola flowers and serve with cream.

COOK'S TIPS

• Small amounts of clear jelly can be frozen on top of cheesecakes or other creamy desserts, but larger jellies need lots of fruit to disguise the loss of clarity as they freeze.
• If you don't have any jelly moulds, recycle small yogurt pots: wash them well before use.

To freeze
At the end of step 4, open-freeze the moulds. Wrap in clingfilm, seal and label. Freeze for up to 2 months.

RUBY RED REFRESHER

Serve this fresh-tasting compote topped with natural yogurt and a sprinkling of muesli or granola for a healthy breakfast.

SERVES 4

PREP: 10 MINUTES, PLUS COOLING TIME

COOK: 2–3 MINUTES

SERVE FROM THE FREEZER: THAW 4 HOURS

2 TSP CORNFLOUR (CORNSTARCH)

55g/2oz CASTER (SUPERFINE) SUGAR

300ml/10FL OZ/1¼ CUPS RED GRAPE JUICE

225g/8oz RED PLUMS, HALVED AND STONED

140g/5oz BLACKBERRIES

225g/8oz SEEDLESS RED GRAPES, HALVED

Put the cornflour and sugar in a saucepan, then gradually mix in the red grape juice until smooth. Heat gently, stirring from time to time, until the sugar has dissolved. Increase the heat and bring to the boil, stirring, until thickened. Add the plums, blackberries and grapes. Simmer for 2–3 minutes, until just tender. Leave to cool.

To serve from frozen
Thaw for 5–6 hours at room temperature, stirring once or twice, or overnight in the fridge.

To freeze
Pack the fruit compote in a plastic container, pour the syrup over and leave to cool completely. Seal and label. Freeze for up to 2 months.

LEMONGRASS, PINEAPPLE AND PASSION FRUIT COMPOTE

SERVES 4
PREP: 15 MINUTES, PLUS COOLING TIME
COOK: 5 MINUTES
SERVE FROM FROZEN: THAW 4 HOURS

2 LEMONGRASS STEMS, SLIT LENGTHWAYS
115g/4oz/½ CUP CASTER (SUPERFINE) SUGAR
1 LARGE PINEAPPLE
GRATED ZEST AND JUICE OF 1 LIME
2 PASSION FRUIT, HALVED

To serve from frozen
Thaw for 7–8 hours at room temperature, stirring once or twice, or 12 hours in the fridge.

If you see pineapples on special offer, freeze one in this easy-to-make lemongrass and lime syrup. This is wonderfully refreshing served with scoops of Coconut and lime sorbet (see page 168).

1. Bruise the lemongrass stems by pressing with the end of a rolling pin or a pestle. Place in a saucepan with the sugar and 600ml/1 pint/2¼ cups water and heat gently, stirring from time to time, until the sugar has dissolved. Increase the heat and simmer for 5 minutes. Leave the syrup to cool for 20 minutes, for the flavours to develop.

2. Meanwhile, cut off the top and bottom of the pineapple. Slice off the skin in strips and remove all the 'eyes'. Slice the fruit into circles, cut in half and cut away the central core.

3. Discard the lemongrass and add the lime zest and juice to the syrup. Using a teaspoon, scoop the seeds from the passion fruit and stir into the syrup.

4. To serve, transfer the pineapple to a glass serving dish, pour the syrup over and leave to cool completely.

To freeze
At the end of step 3, pack the pineapple in a plastic container, pour the syrup over and leave to cool completely. Seal and label. Freeze for up to 2 months.

CHERRY AND LEMON BUTTER
CREPES

These lacy crêpes are spread with lemon butter, then folded and served with a cherry compote. If you can't find cherries, make the compote with blackberries or raspberries and strawberries.

SERVES 4–6

PREP: 20 MINUTES, PLUS 15 MINUTES STANDING

COOK: 15 MINUTES

REHEAT FROM FROZEN: THAW 30 MINUTES; REHEAT 5 MINUTES

Crêpes

115g/4oz/SCANT 1 CUP PLAIN (ALL-PURPOSE) FLOUR

1 EGG, PLUS 1 EGG YOLK

1 TBSP SUNFLOWER OIL, PLUS EXTRA FOR FRYING

250ml/8fl oz/1 CUP MILK

Lemon butter filling

85g/3oz/6 TBSP BUTTER, AT ROOM TEMPERATURE

55g/2oz/½ CUP CASTER (SUPERFINE) SUGAR

GRATED ZEST OF ½ UNWAXED LEMON

Cherry compote

PARED RIND OF ½ UNWAXED LEMON

85g/3oz SCANT ½ CUP CASTER (SUPERFINE) SUGAR

450g/1lb CHERRIES, STONED

1. To make the crêpes, sift the flour into a bowl, add the egg, egg yolk and oil, then gradually whisk in the milk and beat until smooth. Leave to stand for 15 minutes.

2. Meanwhile, make the lemon butter filling: cream all the ingredients together until light and fluffy, then set aside.

3. To make the cherry compote, put the pared lemon rind, sugar and 175ml/6fl oz/¾ cup water in a saucepan and heat gently until the sugar has dissolved, then boil for 3 minutes until syrupy. Add the cherries and cook for 5 minutes, until they are just softened and the juices have begun to colour the syrup. Lift out and discard the lemon rind.

4. To cook the crêpes, whisk the batter once more. Pour a little oil into an 18cm/7in frying pan and heat, then pour out the excess into a small bowl. Pour 2–3 tbsp batter into the pan, tilting it so the batter coats the bottom, then cook until browned on the underside.

5. Loosen the crêpe, then turn over and cook on the second side. Slide out on to a board or large plate. Continue making crêpes and oiling the pan until you have used up all the batter.

6. Spread each crêpe thinly with lemon butter, then fold into four.

7. Arrange half the crêpes in a large frying pan and set over a medium heat for about 5 minutes, turning once, until hot. Repeat with the other half. Reheat the cherry compote.

8. Serve the crêpes in shallow dishes, spoon over the compote and serve, with vanilla ice-cream if you wish.

To serve from frozen

Thaw each two-person portion of crêpes and cherry compote at room temperature for 30 minutes. Separate crêpes and reheat in a frying pan for 4–5 minutes, turning one or twice, until piping hot.

Transfer the cherry compote to a microwaveable dish and cook for 2–3 minutes on full power, stirring once or twice, until piping hot, or reheat in a small saucepan.

To freeze

At the end of step 6, leave the crêpes and compote to cool completely. Pack the crêpes in 2 foil or microwavable dishes. Pack the compote in 2 dishes too. Seal, label and freeze for up to 2 months.

PIES AND TARTS

Make rich, buttery pastry and choose from four different desserts: freeform tarts; a classic lattice-topped tart (see page 126); individual double-crust pies (see page 122); and layered fruit and cream galettes (see page 124).

RICH SWEET PASTRY

If the pastry is difficult to handle, roll it out between 2 sheets of baking parchment or return it to the fridge to chill for a little longer.

225g/8oz/1¾ CUPS PLAIN (ALL-PURPOSE) FLOUR
55g/2oz/½ CUP ICING (CONFECTIONERS') SUGAR
140g/5oz/GENEROUS ½ CUP BUTTER, COLD AND CUBED
3 EGG YOLKS
1 TSP VANILLA EXTRACT

Put the flour in a large mixing bowl, add the icing sugar and butter and rub in the butter until it resembles fine crumbs. Mix the egg yolks with vanilla, add to the flour and mix to form a smooth ball. Wrap in clingfilm (plastic wrap) and chill for 30 minutes.

FREEFORM PLUM AND RASPBERRY TARTS

SERVES 6	
PREP: 25 MINUTES	
COOK: 20–25 MINUTES	
REHEAT FROM FROZEN: 25 MINUTES	

Make up the pastry as described left, and chill.

Stone and slice 350g/12oz red plums and mix with 225g/8oz raspberries, 70g/2½oz/⅓ cup caster (superfine) sugar, 1 tsp cornflour (cornstarch) and the grated zest of 1 unwaxed lemon.

Preheat the oven to 180°C/350°F/Gas Mark 4. Butter 1 large or 2 slightly smaller baking sheets. Divide the pastry into 6 pieces and roll out each piece to a 15–18cm/6–7in diameter circle. Divide the fruit among the pastry circles, leaving a border of 2.5cm/1in. Fold the pastry up and around the fruit, pleating it in soft folds and leaving the centre of the fruit uncovered. Carefully transfer the tarts to the buttered baking sheet. Brush the edges of the pastry with beaten egg and sprinkle with a little caster sugar. Bake for 20–25 minutes.

Leave on the baking sheet to cool for 10 minutes. Serve warm, with custard.

To freeze
After cooking, leave to cool completely. Wrap each tart in foil, then pack in a plastic container. Seal and label. Freeze for up to 4 months.

To serve from frozen
Preheat the oven to 180°C/350°F/Gas Mark 4. Reheat from frozen in the foil for 20 minutes. Open out the foil and bake for another 5 minutes, until piping hot.

DOUBLE-CRUST SUMMER BERRY PIES

SERVES 8	
PREP: 25 MINUTES	
COOK: 20 MINUTES	
SERVE FROM FROZEN: THAW 3–4 HOURS OR REHEAT 25 MINUTES	

Make the pastry as on page 120, omitting the vanilla. Chill for 30 minutes.

In a saucepan, mix 1 tsp cornflour (cornstarch) with 2 tbsp water until smooth. Stir in 25g/1oz/2 tbsp caster (superfine) sugar, then add 225g/8oz strawberries, quartered or halved depending on their size, and 115g/4oz blueberries. Cook gently for 3–4 minutes, stirring, until the fruit just begins to soften and the sauce thickens. Take off the heat and stir in 115g/4oz raspberries. Leave to cool.

Preheat the oven to 180°C/350°F/Gas Mark 4. Butter 8 cups of a muffin tin, or similar-sized foil dishes. Roll out two-thirds of the pastry and use a fluted 9cm/3½in diameter cutter to cut out 8 circles. Use these to line the tins.

Spoon the berry mixture into the pastry cups. Lightly brush the top edges with beaten egg or milk. Roll out the remaining pastry and any trimmings and cut 8 x 7cm/2¾in pastry lids. Press on top of the pies, seal the edges well, then prick the pastry with a fork to let the steam escape. Add tiny pastry decorations made from rerolled pastry trimmings, if liked. Brush with beaten egg and sprinkle with caster (superfine) sugar. Bake for 15–20 minutes, until golden brown.

Leave to cool for 10–15 minutes, then loosen the edges with a knife and turn out on to plates. Drizzle with cream and serve.

To serve from frozen

Preheat the oven to 180°C/350°F/Gas Mark 4. Reheat in the foil for 20 minutes. Open out the foil and cook for another 5 minutes, until hot. Or thaw at room temperature for 3-4 hours in foil.

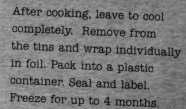

To freeze
After cooking, leave to cool completely. Remove from the tins and wrap individually in foil. Pack into a plastic container. Seal and label. Freeze for up to 4 months.

APPLE AND BLACKBERRY GALETTES

SERVES 8	
PREP: 20 MINUTES	
COOK: 8–10 MINUTES	
SERVE FROM FROZEN: THAW 3–4 HOURS	

Make the pastry as described on page 120, replacing the vanilla with the grated zest of 1 unwaxed lemon. Chill for 30 minutes.

Preheat the oven to 180°C/350°F/Gas Mark 4. Roll out and cut out 16 x 7.5cm/3in circles, using a fluted pastry cutter. Reroll the trimmings and cut out more circles until all the pastry has been used. Place on greased baking sheets, prick with a fork and sprinkle with a little caster (superfine) sugar. Bake for 8–10 minutes, until pale golden brown. Leave to cool on the baking sheet.

Meanwhile, core, peel and dice 2 dessert apples. Place in a saucepan with 115g/4oz/1 cup blackberries, the juice of 1 lemon and 4 tbsp caster (superfine) sugar. Cover and simmer for 5 minutes, until just cooked. Mash any large pieces of fruit and leave to cool.

To serve, sandwich 2 galettes with a spoonful of crème fraîche from a 250ml/8fl oz/1 cup pot and a generous spoonful of the fruit compote. Dust the tops with sifted icing sugar.

To serve from frozen

Thaw the galettes and fruit at room temperature for 3–4 hours. Sandwich the galettes with crème fraîche and fruit compote and dust with sifted icing (confectioners') sugar.

To freeze

After cooking, but before sandwiching, leave the galettes and fruit compote to cool completely. Pack in separate plastic containers, seal and label. Freeze for up to 2 months.

PEACH AND VANILLA
LATTICE TART

SERVES 6–8	
PREP: 30 MINUTES	
COOK: 25–30 MINUTES	
COOK FROM FROZEN: 55–60 MINUTES	

Make the pastry as described on page 120. Chill for 30 minutes. Halve 6 peaches, remove the stones, and cut into thick slices. Toss with 1 tsp vanilla extract, then sprinkle over 70g/2½oz/1/3 cup caster (superfine) sugar and 1 tsp cornflour (cornstarch) and toss gently until evenly coated.

Preheat the oven to 180°C/350°F/Gas Mark 4. Butter a 24cm/9½in fluted loose-bottomed tart tin. Roll out two-thirds of the pastry on a lightly floured surface until a little larger than the tin. Lift the pastry over a rolling pin and unroll over the tin. Press into the bottom and up the sides, then trim a little above the rim of the tin. Add the trimmings to the reserved pastry.

Spoon the peach mixture into the pastry shell in a single layer. Roll out the remaining pastry to a rectangle that is a little longer than the diameter of the tart and cut out long strips, 2.5cm/1in wide. Arrange the strips over the top of the tart, sticking them to the edge of the tart with beaten egg or egg white. Reroll the trimmings if necessary, until the top of the tart is covered with a lattice of pastry, leaving the lattice ends overhanging the edge of the tart. Brush the lattice lightly with beaten egg and sprinkle with caster (superfine) sugar. Place on a baking sheet and bake for 25–30 minutes, until the pastry is golden brown. Trim off the overhanging ends of pastry from the lattice top.

If not freezing, cook the tart for another 10 minutes, covering the top loosely with foil to prevent the pastry from over-browning. Leave for 15 minutes before slicing. Serve with crème fraîche.

To serve from frozen

Preheat the oven to 180°C/350°F/Gas Mark 4. Unwrap the tart, loosely cover the top with foil and bake the frozen tart for 55-60 minutes, removing the foil for the last 10 minutes.

To freeze

After cooking, leave the tart to cool completely. Wrap the tart tin in foil, seal and label. Freeze for up to 4 months

SAFFRON-SPICED PEAR TARTE TATIN

This topsy-turvy French-style puff pastry tart is made with pears cooked in a buttery aromatic syrup, flavoured with saffron, cardamom, cinnamon and ginger. Freeze it partly made, then bake when needed and serve with crème fraîche.

SERVES 6

PREP: 25 MINUTES

COOK: 25–30 MINUTES

COOK FROM THE FREEZER: THAW 2–3 HOURS,
    COOK 35–40 MINUTES

LARGE PINCH OF SAFFRON THREADS

1 TBSP BOILING WATER

85g/3oz/6 TBSP UNSALTED BUTTER

115g/4oz/½ CUP CASTER (SUPERFINE) SUGAR

3 CARDAMOM PODS, CRUSHED

1 CINNAMON STICK, BROKEN INTO LARGE SHARDS

2cm/¾in PIECE FRESH GINGER, PEELED AND
    CUT INTO TINY STRIPS

1 UNWAXED LEMON, RIND PARED AND CUT INTO THIN
    STRIPS, PLUS JUICE

6 MEDIUM PEARS

250g/9oz CHILLED PUFF PASTRY

PLAIN (ALL-PURPOSE) FLOUR, FOR DUSTING

1. Put the saffron in a cup, pour over the boiling water and leave to soak for a few minutes. Put the butter and sugar in a large frying pan, then add the cardamom pods and seeds, cinnamon stick, ginger and lemon rind. Heat gently until the butter has melted, swirling if needed but not stirring, then take off the heat.

2. Peel, quarter and core the pears and toss them with the lemon juice. Stir the saffron threads and soaking water into the frying pan, then add the pears and lemon juice, spreading evenly.

3. Cook the pears over a medium–low heat for 5–8 minutes, until they are just beginning to soften (the timing depends on how ripe they are). Turn several times so that they cook and colour evenly in the saffron syrup.

4. Increase the heat and boil the syrup and pears for 2 minutes, until the syrup begins to thicken.

5. Arrange the pears, spices and syrup in a 20cm/8in round, 5cm/2in deep, metal pie plate, with the curved sides of the pears facing downward and most of the spices, lemon and ginger strips on the bottom of the dish. Leave to cool.

Recipe continues...

FREEZING TIP
So that the pie plate is not out of action while the tart is in the freezer, line the pie plate with foil and tuck the ends loosely over the sides of the dish. Add the pears, syrup and pastry, then freeze until firm. Lift out the foil and tart, wrap completely in foil, seal, label and put back in the freezer for up to 2 months. To serve, put the foil parcel back into the metal pie plate to bake.

TARTE TATIN
...CONTINUED

6. Roll out the pastry on a lightly floured surface until a little larger than the top of the pie plate. Trim it to a neat 25cm/10in circle using a dinner plate as a guide, then lay over the pears and tuck the edges of the pastry down the sides of the pie plate. Prick the top with a fork to allow steam to escape.

7. To serve now, preheat the oven to 200°C/400°F/Gas Mark 6. Cook for 25–30 minutes, until the pastry is well risen and golden brown and the syrup is bubbling around the sides. Leave to stand for 5 minutes. Loosen the edge, cover the pie plate with a serving plate, invert the tart, then remove the pie plate. Slice and serve with crème fraîche.

ALSO TRY
Instead of pears, use apple quarters, and flavour the syrup with a slit vanilla pod and the grated zest and juice of ½ orange and ½ unwaxed lemon instead of cardamom, cinnamon, ginger and lemon. Pour over a little flaming brandy or Calvados as you serve the tart.

To serve from frozen
Thaw at room temperature for 2–3 hours. Preheat the oven to 200°C/400°F/Gas Mark 6. Remove the wrapping and cook for 35–40 minutes, until the pastry is risen and golden brown and the syrup is bubbling around the sides. Leave to stand for 5 minutes. Invert onto a serving plate as above.

To freeze
At the end of step 6, wrap the pie plate in clingfilm (plastic wrap), seal and label. Freeze for up to 2 months.

PLUM
FRANGIPANE TART

A crisp buttery pastry with a sweet, softly set, almond filling is delicious with the slightly sharp plums; this also works well with sliced pears or apples. If you don't have a rectangular loose-bottomed tart tin, improvise with a roasting tin with the same base measurement.

MAKES 12 PIECES
PREP: 30 MINUTES
CHILL: 20–30 MINUTES
COOK: 50–55 MINUTES
SERVE FROM FROZEN: THAW UNCOOKED TART FOR
    2 HOURS, COOK 45–50 MINUTES; THAW COOKED
    TART FOR 2 HOURS, REHEAT FOR 10 MINUTES

Pastry

225g/8oz/1¾ CUPS PLAIN (ALL-PURPOSE) FLOUR, PLUS
    EXTRA FOR DUSTING
55g/2OZ/¼ CUP CASTER (SUPERFINE) SUGAR
115g/4oz/½ CUP BUTTER, COLD AND CUBED

Frangipane plum filling

140g/5oz/GENEROUS ½ CUP BUTTER, AT
    ROOM TEMPERATURE
140g/5oz/SCANT ¾ CUP CASTER (SUPERFINE) SUGAR
140g/5oz/1½ CUPS GROUND ALMONDS
2 TBSP PLAIN (ALL-PURPOSE) FLOUR
2 EGGS, BEATEN
A FEW DROPS OF ALMOND EXTRACT (OPTIONAL)
450g/1lb RED PLUMS, STONED AND SLICED
3 TBSP SLIVERED ALMONDS
ICING (CONFECTIONERS') SUGAR, TO SERVE

1. To make the pastry, put the flour, sugar and butter in a bowl and rub in the butter with your fingertips until it resembles fine crumbs. Gradually add about 3 tbsp cold water, until you can squeeze the crumbs together to make a smooth dough.

2. Knead a little on a lightly floured surface, then roll out to a little larger than a 28 x 18 x 4cm/11 x 7 x 1½in fluted loose-bottomed tart tin or cake tin. Lift the pastry over a rolling pin, unroll over the tin and press gently into the corners. Trim a little above the top of the tin to allow for shrinkage. Prick the pastry with a fork, then chill for 20–30 minutes.

3. Preheat the oven to 190°C/375°F/Gas Mark 5. Line the pastry shell with baking parchment and dried beans, then bake for 15 minutes. Remove the paper and beans and cook for another 5 minutes, until the pastry is crisp. Leave to cool. Reduce the oven temperature to 180°C/350°F/Gas Mark 4 if serving now.

4. Meanwhile, make the filling by creaming the butter and sugar together, using a wooden spoon or electric mixer, until light and fluffy. Gradually beat in alternate spoonfuls of the ground almonds and flour with the beaten eggs, until smooth. Stir in the almond essence, if using. Spoon the frangipane mixture into the pastry shell and spread evenly. Sprinkle the plums and almonds over the top.

5. Bake for 30–35 minutes, until the frangipane is golden. Leave to cool for 20 minutes. Remove from the tin and cut into pieces.

6. Serve warm, dusted with sifted icing sugar just before serving. Alternatively, wrap in foil or pack in a plastic container and chill for up to 2 days.

To serve from frozen

Thaw uncooked tart at room temperature for 2 hours. Remove wrappings and bake in a preheated oven at 180°C/350°F/Gas Mark 4 for 45-50 minutes, covering with foil after 30 minutes. Or thaw cooked tart for 2 hours and reheat in foil for 10 minutes.

To freeze

After step 4, wrap the uncooked tart, still in its tin, in clingfilm or foil, seal and label. Or wrap baked and cooled pieces of tart in foil and pack in a plastic container. Seal, label and freeze for up to 2 months.

RASPBERRY AND LEMON CURD CHEESECAKE

SERVES 8–10

PREP: 25 MINUTES

COOK: 35–45 MINUTES

SERVE FROM FROZEN: THAW 13–19 HOURS

250g/9oz DIGESTIVE BISCUITS (GRAHAM CRACKERS)
85g/3oz/6 TBSP BUTTER
600g/1lb 5oz/2½ CUPS CREAM CHEESE
115g/4oz/½ CUP CASTER (SUPERFINE) SUGAR
1 TBSP CORNFLOUR (CORNSTARCH)
GRATED ZEST OF 1 UNWAXED LEMON
4 EGGS
175ml/6fl oz/¾ CUP DOUBLE (HEAVY) CREAM
140g/5oz FRESH RASPBERRIES, PLUS EXTRA TO DECORATE
3 TBSP LEMON CURD
ICING SUGAR, SIFTED, TO DECORATE

To freeze
At the end of step 5, remove the cheesecake from the tin, wrap in clingfilm, then pack in a plastic container. Seal and label. Freeze for up to 2 months.

To serve from frozen
Remove the clingfilm and put the cheesecake back into the plastic container. Thaw for 12–18 hours in the fridge, then leave at room temperature for 1–2 hours before serving.

Cheesecakes freeze well and can, if you like, be topped with a thin layer of crème fraîche when thawed. This summery raspberry cheesecake would be delicious served with a drizzle of raspberry sauce (see page 164), or lightly dusted with sifted icing sugar and decorated with a few extra raspberries.

1. Preheat the oven to 180°C/350°F/Gas Mark 4. Crush the biscuits to fine crumbs in a food processor or in a plastic bag using a rolling pin. Melt the butter in a saucepan, then stir in the crumbs. Tip into a buttered 23cm/9in springform tin and press the biscuits over the bottom in an even layer. Bake for 5 minutes.

2. Take the base out of the oven and reduce the oven temperature to 150°C/300°F/Gas Mark 2.

3. Put the cream cheese, sugar, cornflour and lemon zest in a food processor or large mixing bowl and beat until just smooth. Beat in the eggs one by one, then gradually beat in the cream until smooth. Mix 3 tbsp of this mixture with the lemon curd, and set aside.

4. Pour the remaining cream cheese mixture on to the biscuit base. Sprinkle the raspberries on top, then drop small spoonfuls of the lemon curd mixture randomly among the raspberries. Bake for 35–45 minutes, until the cheesecake is just beginning to turn golden around the edges and the centre is just set, with a soft wobble.

5. Turn off the oven and open the door slightly. Leave the cheesecake to cool in the oven for 2 hours (it will crack as it cools). Transfer to the fridge until completely cold and firm.

6. To serve, loosen the edge of the cheesecake, remove from the tin, put on a serving plate and decorate with extra raspberries and a dusting of sifted icing sugar

FREEZING TIP
The cheesecake could also be cut into slices before freezing. Interleave the slices with strips of baking parchment, then wrap in clingfilm (plastic wrap) and pack in a plastic container. Thaw slices in the fridge for 4 hours, then for 1 hour at room temperature.

QUICK CHEATS PUDS

Bags of frozen summer fruits – either home-frozen or from the supermarket – make a great base for a speedy dessert. Thaw them in minutes in the microwave or use straight them from the freezer.

CHEATS' SUMMER BERRY SORBET

SERVES 4

PREP: 10 MINUTES

Put 500g/1lb 2oz frozen mixed summer berries in a food processor with 6 tbsp undiluted blackcurrant cordial and 4 tbsp caster (superfine) sugar. Pulse in short bursts until the fruits begin to break up. Continue until the mixture is smooth and thick. Add the leaves from 2 sprigs of mint and mix until finely chopped. Spoon into glasses and serve, or stir through a few spoonfuls of honey-flavoured Greek-style yogurt for a rippled effect. Serve immediately while the fruits are still frozen, or return to the freezer to firm up some more.

VERY BERRY JELLY

SERVES 4–6

PREP: 10 MINUTES PLUS 1 HOUR CHILLING

Pour 150ml/5fl oz/⅔ cup red grape juice into a heatproof bowl and sprinkle over 2 x 12g sachets of powdered gelatine. Leave to stand for 5 minutes so that the juice absorbs all the powder, then warm the bowl in a saucepan of gently simmering water for 4–5 minutes, until clear and liquid. Meanwhile, tip 500g/1lb 2 oz frozen mixed summer berries into dessert glasses. Stir 55g/2oz/4 tbsp caster (superfine) sugar into the gelatine mixture until dissolved, then mix in an extra 300ml/10fl oz/1¼ cups grape juice. Pour over the frozen fruits, stir and chill for at least 1 hour, or until set.

MIXED BERRY ETON MESS (PICTURED PAGE 113)

SERVES 4

PREP: 10 MINUTES

Microwave 350g/12oz frozen mixed summer berries for 2–3 minutes on full power, until soft enough to mash. Leave to stand for 5 minutes. Whip 250ml/8fl oz/1 cup double (heavy) cream until it forms soft swirls, fold in 250g/9oz/1 cup natural yogurt and 2 tbsp lemon curd, then crumble 4 ready-made meringue nests and fold in. Drop alternate spoonfuls of the cream mixture and mashed berries into 4 wine glasses, ending with a spoonful of the berries and a little extra crumbled meringue. Serve immediately.

QUICK CHEATS
...CONTINUED

BLUEBERRY HOTCAKES

SERVES 4

PREP: 10 MINUTES

COOK: 10 MINUTES

Mix 175g/6oz/1½ cups self-raising flour with
½ tsp bicarbonate of soda (baking soda) in a
bowl. Add 2 beaten eggs, 140g/5oz/⅔ cup
natural yogurt, 150ml/5fl oz/⅔ cup milk and
the grated zest of ½ unwaxed lemon. Whisk
together until smooth, then stir in 115g/4oz
frozen blueberries.

Grease a large frying pan with a little sunflower oil
and place over a medium heat. Drop spoonfuls of
the batter, well spaced apart, into the pan and cook
for a few minutes, until bubbles begin to appear on
the surface and the undersides of the pancakes are
golden. Turn over and cook the second side until
golden and the juices are beginning to run from
the blueberries. Keep warm while you cook the
remaining batter. Serve hot with a little butter and a
drizzle of maple syrup.

SUMMER BERRIES
WITH WHITE
CHOCOLATE FONDUE

SERVES 4

PREP: 10 MINUTES

COOK: 4–5 MINUTES

Partly thaw 350g/12oz frozen mixed summer
berries in the microwave for 2 minutes on full power,
then leave to stand while making the fondue. Pour
125ml/4fl oz/½ cup double (heavy) cream into a
small saucepan, add 1 tbsp runny honey and 4 tbsp
medium-dry white wine and bring just to the boil,
stirring. Add 115g/4oz white chocolate, broken into
pieces, and stir over a very low heat until the chocolate
has just melted. Spoon the berries into shallow glass
dishes and pour the hot fondue over the top: the heat
will finish thawing the fruit. Decorate with grated or
shaved white chocolate and serve immediately.

LEMON POSSET
WITH CHERRIES

SERVES 4

PREP: 5 MINUTES, PLUS 30 MINUTES CHILLING

COOK: 3–4 MINUTES

Pour 450ml/16fl oz/2 cups double (heavy) cream
into a saucepan, add 125g/4½oz/generous ½ cup
caster (superfine) sugar and bring to the boil, stirring,
until the sugar has dissolved; cook for 1 minute. Take
off the heat and stir in the grated zest of 1 unwaxed
lemon and 3 tbsp lemon juice. Leave to stand for a
minute or two to thicken slightly. Divide 350g/12oz
frozen stoned cherries between 4 glasses, pour in the
hot cream mixture and leave to cool for 15 minutes: the
frozen cherries will speed up chilling and the warmth
from the custard will thaw them. Transfer to the fridge
for 30 minutes or so before serving.

CAKES
& BAKES

CAKES & BAKES

There's something special about offering visitors a slice of homemade cake, but when we are expecting guests it's often hard to find the time for that extra bit of cooking. However, it can be calming to spend an hour or so baking, and it's immensely rewarding. Why not make a large cake instead of a small one, and freeze some of it in convenient, easy-to-thaw pieces? Alternatively, cookie dough can be sliced and frozen, ready to bake straight from the freezer in a matter of minutes.

Individual chocolate fondants can be cooked straight from the freezer and a rich, creamy coffee sauce for them is frozen in sections of an ice-cube tray so you can reheat as many portions as you need and enjoy them with a scoop of ice-cream. Maple pecan pie can also be reheated straight from the freezer – and it makes a lovely gift, with a more personal touch than flowers.

Celebrate a special occasion or birthday with a three-tiered dark chocolate cake. Make it a week or even a month in advance, but check that there is space in your freezer before you begin. Personalize the top with a piped chocolate message or sprinkle with chocolate curls or fresh raspberries. Cup cakes can also be personalized, or to celebrate a new baby why not colour the buttercream pale pink or blue? You can take them to work or school while still frozen and they will have thawed by mid-morning.

If you are not warming cakes in the oven, they are best thawed at room temperature, as they tend to heat unevenly in the microwave. There may be a small amount of condensation, but if you uncover the cakes for 30 minutes before serving this will disappear.

CREAMY MINT CHOCOLATE CAKE

This dark chocolate cake, layered with white chocolate cream and swirled extravagantly with a rich, dark chocolate frosting definitely has the wow factor. The cake is made by simply beating all the ingredients together – what could be easier? It can be frozen decorated, ready for a special celebration.

SERVES 20

PREP: 45 MINUTES

COOK: ABOUT 1 HOUR

SERVE FROM FROZEN: THAW 19 HOURS

SUNFLOWER OIL FOR GREASING
300g/10½oz/1¼ CUPS SOFT MARGARINE
300g/10½oz/1½ CUPS CASTER (SUPERFINE) SUGAR
250g/9oz/2 CUPS SELF-RAISING FLOUR
70g/2½oz/½ CUP UNSWEETENED COCOA POWDER
1 TSP BAKING POWDER
5 EGGS, BEATEN
DARK CHOCOLATE SHAVINGS, TO DECORATE

White chocolate filling

115g/4oz WHITE CHOCOLATE, BROKEN INTO PIECES
250ml/8fl oz/1 CUP DOUBLE (HEAVY) CREAM
3 TBSP FINELY CHOPPED FRESH MINT
200g/7oz/1 CUP FRESH RASPBERRIES

Dark chocolate frosting

250ml/8fl oz/1 CUP DOUBLE (HEAVY) CREAM
200g/7oz DARK CHOCOLATE, BROKEN INTO PIECES

1. Preheat the oven to 180°C/350°F/Gas Mark 4. Lightly brush a 23cm/9in springform cake tin with oil and line the bottom with baking parchment.

2. Put the margarine, sugar, flour, cocoa, baking powder and eggs in a bowl and beat with an electric mixer until smooth.

3. Spoon the cake mixture into the prepared tin and smooth the surface with a spatula. Bake for 55–60 minutes, or until well risen, the top has cracked slightly and a skewer inserted into the centre comes out clean. Check after 30 minutes and cover the top loosely with foil if it is browning too quickly.

4. Leave to cool in the tin for 10 minutes, then loosen the edge. Remove from the tin and transfer to a wire rack to cool completely.

5. To make the filling, put the white chocolate in a heatproof bowl set over a saucepan of gently simmering water and leave for 5 minutes, until melted. Stir until smooth and leave to cool. Whip the cream until soft peaks form, then fold in the melted white chocolate and chopped mint.

6. Peel the lining paper away from the cake and slice the cake into three thin layers. Sandwich the layers together with the white chocolate mixture and the raspberries. Transfer to a serving plate if serving now or a square of baking parchment if freezing.

Recipe continues…

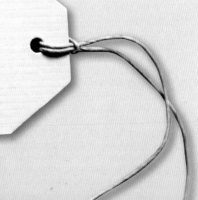

To freeze

At the end of step 7, carefully transfer the cake on the paper to the lid of a large plastic container. Cover with the upturned container, seal and label. Freeze for up to 2 months.

CHOCOLATE CAKE
...CONTINUED

7. To make the frosting, pour the cream into a saucepan, bring just to the boil, then take the pan off the heat, add the dark chocolate and leave to stand for 5 minutes, until the chocolate has melted. Stir until smooth. Leave to cool for 5–15 minutes, until just beginning to thicken, then stir once more. Spread a thin layer of frosting all over the cake. Spoon the remaining frosting onto the cake and spread evenly over the top and sides, then swirl with a round-bladed knife. Decorate with chocolate shavings (made using a vegetable peeler) or a piped melted chocolate message.

8. Chill until ready to serve.

ALSO TRY

Black Forest-style cake – omit the chopped mint in the white chocolate filling. Sandwich the cakes together with the filling and 250g/9oz (drained weight) canned pitted cherries. You could also drizzle the sponge with a few tablespoons of Kirsch or brandy before you sandwich the cakes together.

Chocolate truffle cake – omit the white chocolate filling and make double the amount of dark chocolate frosting to sandwich and cover the cake. Drizzle the sponge with a little brandy or rum as you sandwich the cakes together.

To serve from frozen

Peel off the paper. Transfer the cake to a serving plate. Defrost for 18 hours in the fridge, uncovered, to allow the condensation to evaporate. Take out of the fridge 1 hour before serving.

BEETROOT AND GINGER DRIZZLE CAKE

MAKES 24 SMALL SQUARES
PREP: 25 MINUTES
COOK: 30–35 MINUTES
SERVE FROM FROZEN: THAW 2–3 HOURS

3 EGGS

150ml/5fl oz/⅔ CUP SUNFLOWER OIL

175g/6oz/¾ CUP LIGHT BROWN SUGAR

225g/8oz/SCANT 2 CUPS SELF-RAISING FLOUR

1 TSP BAKING POWDER

3 TSP GROUND GINGER

GRATED ZEST OF 1 ORANGE

175g/6oz BEETROOT (BEETS), COOKED WITHOUT VINEGAR,
    COARSELY GRATED

40g/1½oz PRESERVED GINGER, DRAINED AND
    FINELY CHOPPED

2 TBSP SUNFLOWER SEEDS

1 TBSP PUMPKIN SEEDS (OPTIONAL)

Orange drizzle

140g/5oz/SCANT ¾ CUP GRANULATED SUGAR

3 TBSP FRESHLY SQUEEZED ORANGE JUICE

The inclusion of grated beetroot in this cake may seem surprising, but it adds moistness and combines with the sunflower oil to give a richness that you would normally associate with butter.

1. Preheat the oven to 180°C/350°F/Gas Mark 4. Line an 18 x 28cm/7 x 11in roasting or cake pan with a large piece of baking parchment, snipping diagonally into the corners, then press into the pan so that the base and sides are lined.

2. Put the eggs, oil and sugar in a large bowl and whisk together briefly. Sift the flour, baking powder and ground ginger into the bowl and whisk until just mixed. Add the orange zest and beetroot and mix until just smooth. Pour the mixture into the prepared pan and sprinkle with the preserved ginger, sunflower seeds and pumpkin seeds, if using. Bake for 30–35 minutes, until the cake is well risen and a skewer inserted into the centre comes out clean.

3. Meanwhile, for the drizzle, mix the granulated sugar and orange juice together. As soon as the cake comes of the oven, lift it out of the pan, place on a wire rack still in the paper and spoon the syrup over the top. Leave to cool.

4. To serve, peel away the paper and cut the cake into small squares.

CARROT CAKE

Replace the grated beetroot with grated raw carrot and add 55g/2oz/scant ½ cup walnut pieces. Replace 1 tsp of the ground ginger with 1 tsp ground cinnamon. Omit the preserved ginger and the seeds. Spread the top of the cooled cake with 200g/7oz/generous ¾ cup cream cheese mixed with 55g/2oz/½ cup icing (confectioners') sugar and the grated zest of ½ orange. Sprinkle with a few walnut pieces and freeze as described.

To freeze
At the end of step 3, cut the cake into three pieces, remove the lining paper and wrap each individually in foil or clingfilm (plastic wrap), seal and label. Freeze for up to 2 months.

To serve from frozen
Take out as many wrapped cake parcels as you need. Thaw at room temperature for 2-3 hours, then unwrap and cut into squares.

COOK'S TIP
Make an apple, ginger and lemon drizzle cake. Omit the beetroot and add the same weight of peeled and coarsely grated dessert apple. Flavour the cake mixture with the finely grated zest of 1 unwaxed lemon instead of orange. For the drizzle, replace the orange juice with lemon juice. Omit the seeds.

CITRUS CUPCAKES

Light sponge cakes with a hint of orange and lemon, decorated with a swirl of buttercream. For a birthday celebration, add candles to the cakes.

MAKES 12

PREP: 25 MINUTES

COOK: 15 MINUTES

SERVE FROM FROZEN: THAW 2 HOURS

115g/4oz/½ CUP BUTTER, AT ROOM TEMPERATURE

115g/4oz/GENEROUS ½ CUP CASTER (SUPERFINE) SUGAR

115g/4oz/1 CUP SELF-RAISING FLOUR

2 EGGS

GRATED ZEST OF ½ UNWAXED LEMON

GRATED ZEST OF ½ ORANGE

12–24 SMALL SUGAR FLOWERS, TO DECORATE

EDIBLE GLITTER OR SPRINKLES, TO DECORATE (OPTIONAL)

Buttercream frosting

115g/4oz/½ CUP BUTTER, AT ROOM TEMPERATURE

225g/8oz/2 CUPS ICING (CONFECTIONERS') SUGAR

GRATED ZEST OF ½ UNWAXED LEMON AND 1 TBSP JUICE

GRATED ZEST OF ½ ORANGE AND 1 TBSP JUICE

1. Preheat the oven to 180°C/350°F/Gas Mark 4. Put 12 paper cake case into a muffin or bun tin.

2. Put the butter, sugar, flour, eggs and lemon and orange zest into a bowl or food processor and beat until smooth. Divide among the cake cases and cook for about 15 minutes, until well risen and golden brown and the tops of the cakes spring back when lightly pressed with a fingertip.

3. Take the cakes out of the tin and transfer to a wire rack to cool.

4. To make the frosting, put the butter and icing sugar into a food processor or mixing bowl, add the fruit zests and juices, then beat until smooth. Spoon into a large piping bag fitted with a star tube, then pipe whirls of buttercream over each cake. Add the sugar flowers or edible glitter, if using.

ALSO TRY

• For chocolate capuccino cupcakes, replace 15g/½oz/1½ tbsp of the flour with the same amount of unsweetened cocoa powder, omit the fruit zest and add 2 tsp instant coffee dissolved in 2 tsp boiling water. Omit the fruit zest and juice from the frosting and flavour with 1 tsp vanilla extract; dust with finely grated chocolate.

• For small children you may prefer to omit the fruit zest and juice. Instead, flavour the cakes with 1 tsp vanilla extract. For the frosting, replace the fruit zest and juice with 1 tsp vanilla extract and 2 tbsp milk. Decorate with milk and white chocolate buttons or other tiny sweets.

To freeze
Pack in a single layer in a plastic container. Cover, seal and label. Freeze for up to 2 months.

To serve from frozen
Take out as many cakes as required and put on a plate. Cover with a food net and thaw at room temperature for 2 hours.

BLUEBERRY
AND WHITE CHOCOLATE
MUFFINS

MAKES 12	
PREP: 15 MINUTES	
COOK: 15–20 MINUTES	
SERVE FROM FROZEN: THAW 2–3 HOURS, OR 30 SECONDS IN THE MICROWAVE, OR 8–10 MINUTES IN THE OVEN	

125ml/4fl oz/½ CUP SUNFLOWER OIL
140g/5oz/⅔ CUP NATURAL YOGURT
2 EGGS, BEATEN
1 TSP VANILLA EXTRACT
250g/9oz/2 CUPS SELF-RAISING FLOUR
1 TSP BICARBONATE OF SODA (BAKING SODA)
115g/4oz/GENEROUS ½ CUP CASTER (SUPERFINE) SUGAR
140g/5oz/1 CUP BLUEBERRIES
115g/4oz WHITE CHOCOLATE, ROUGHLY CHOPPED

To serve from frozen

Preheat the oven to 150°C/300°F/Gas Mark 2. Take as many muffins from the freezer as you need, unwrap the clingfilm and loosely wrap in foil. Reheat from frozen for 8-10 minutes, until hot through, or loosen the clingfilm and microwave one at a time in 10-second bursts for 30 seconds on full power. Leave to stand for 2 minutes before serving. Keep a watchful eye, as the muffins can easily develop brown overcooked patches in the microwave.

Take just one or two of these yummy muffins from the freezer, warm in the microwave or oven and serve with a cup of coffee or tea as a mid-morning treat. Or add to a packed lunchbox and they will have thawed by lunchtime if kept at room temperature.

1. Preheat the oven to 190°C/375°F/Gas Mark 5. Put 12 paper muffin cases into a 12-hole muffin tin.

2. Using a fork, mix the oil, yogurt, eggs and vanilla together in a bowl. Put the flour, bicarbonate of soda and sugar in a large bowl. Add the wet ingredients to the dry and fork together briefly until just mixed: don't worry if there are a few floury specks – the briefer the mixing the lighter the muffins will be.

3. Add the blueberries and chocolate and stir briefly, then spoon the mixture into the paper cases. Bake for 15–20 minutes, until well risen and golden brown. Serve warm from the oven.

ALSO TRY

• Prune and vanilla – omit the blueberries and white chocolate; add 140g/5oz/scant 1 cup ready-to-eat (plumped) roughly chopped prunes.
• Banana and pecan – omit the blueberries and white chocolate; instead of the yogurt, add 2 medium ripe mashed bananas and 55g/2oz/½ cup roughly crushed pecan nuts.
• Apricot and muesli – omit the blueberries and white chocolate; add 115g/4oz/scant 1 cup ready-to-eat dried (plumped) chopped apricots and 85g/3oz/1 cup breakfast muesli.
• Spiced cranberry and orange – omit the white chocolate and blueberries; add 85g/3oz/⅔ cup dried cranberries, grated zest of 1 large orange, 1 tsp ground cinnamon and ½ tsp ground mixed spice (pumpkin pie spice).

To freeze
Leave the muffins to cool completely, then wrap individually in clingfilm and pack in a plastic container, seal and label. Freeze for up to 2 months.

TRIPLE CHOC COOKIES

MAKES 18–20

PREP: 20 MINUTES, PLUS 30 MINUTES CHILLING

COOK: 12–15 MINUTES

COOK FROM FROZEN: 15–18 MINUTES

250g/9oz/2 CUPS PLAIN (ALL-PURPOSE) FLOUR
115g/4oz/GENEROUS ½ CUP CASTER (SUPERFINE) SUGAR
175g/6oz/¾ CUP BUTTER, COLD AND CUBED
1 TSP VANILLA EXTRACT
55g/2oz DARK CHOCOLATE, ROUGHLY CHOPPED
55g/2oz MILK CHOCOLATE, ROUGHLY CHOPPED
55g/2oz WHITE CHOCOLATE, ROUGHLY CHOPPED

To freeze

At the end of step 4, interleave the raw dough slices with squares of baking parchment and stack in a plastic container. Seal, label and freeze for up to 2 months.

To serve from frozen

Preheat the oven to 180°C/350°F/ Gas Mark 4. Take out as many slices as you need, place on an ungreased baking sheet and bake for 15-18 minutes, until golden brown around the edges. Leave to cool for a few minutes, then loosen the cookies with a palette knife and transfer to a wire rack.

Welcome the kids home from school with the smell of freshly baked biscuits, or impress your friends when they pop in for coffee. The dough can be sliced and frozen; just take out as many biscuits as you need and cook straight from the freezer.

1. Put the flour and sugar in a bowl, add the butter and rub in with fingertips until it resembles fine crumbs.

2. Add the vanilla and chocolates, stir and continue mixing until the crumbs and chocolate begin to stick together, then squeeze gently to make a ball.

3. Knead the dough lightly until smooth, then place on a piece of baking parchment and roll into a log about 25cm/10in long and 5cm/2in diameter. Wrap the parchment around the dough, twist the ends together and chill for 30 minutes.

4. Unwrap and cut into 18–20 slices, about 1cm/½in thick.

5. To cook now, preheat the oven to 180°C/350°F/Gas Mark 4. Arrange the slices on a non-stick ungreased baking sheet and bake for 12–15 minutes, until lightly browned.

ALSO TRY

• Tropical coconut – omit the vanilla and chocolate; add the grated zest of 1 lime and 1 orange and 55g/2oz/generous ½ cup desiccated coconut.
• Sultana and lemon – omit the vanilla and chocolate; add 55g/2oz/5 tbsp sultanas (golden raisins), 1 tsp caraway seeds and the grated zest of ½ unwaxed lemon. Slice, then sprinkle with a little caster (superfine) sugar.
• Ginger and oat – omit the vanilla, chocolate and 25g/1oz/3 tbsp flour; add 55g/2oz/scant ¾ cup rolled oats and 25g/1oz roughly chopped and drained preserved ginger. Slice, then sprinkle with demerara (raw brown) sugar.
• Malted milk and milk choc chip – omit the vanilla, dark and white chocolates and 25g/1oz/3 tbsp flour; add 3 tbsp malted milk powder (for hot milky bedtime drinks, such as Horlicks and Ovaltine) and increase the milk chocolate to 140g/5oz.
• Almond – omit the vanilla and chocolate and 55g/2oz/ ½ cup flour; add 55g/2oz/½ cup ground almonds and a few drops of almond extract. Slice, then sprinkle with flaked almonds. Dust with sifted icing (confectioners') sugar after baking.

SALTED HAZELNUT FUDGE BROWNIES

MAKES 24 SMALL SQUARES
PREP: 25 MINUTES
COOK: 25–30 MINUTES
SERVE FROM FROZEN: 1 MINUTE IN THE MICROWAVE, OR THAW FOR 2 HOURS AND REHEAT FOR 10 MINUTES

100g/3½oz/¾ CUP BLANCHED HAZELNUTS
½ TSP COARSE SALT
250g/9oz DARK CHOCOLATE, BROKEN INTO PIECES
175g/6oz/¾ CUP BUTTER
3 EGGS, BEATEN
225g/8oz/GENEROUS 1 CUP LIGHT BROWN SUGAR
85g/3OZ/⅔ CUP SELF-RAISING FLOUR
1 TSP BAKING POWDER
100g/3½oz CREAM FUDGE, ROUGHLY CHOPPED

To freeze
At the end of step 5, cut the brownie into quarters and wrap each piece in foil. Seal, label and freeze for up to 2 months.

To serve from frozen
Microwave a quarter at a time, unwrapped, in 20-second bursts for up to 1 minute on full power. Leave to stand for 5 minutes, then cut into small squares. Alternatively, take out as many pieces as you need and thaw for 2 hours. Preheat the oven to 160°C/325°F/Gas Mark 3, warm the brownie, still wrapped loosely in foil, for 10 minutes. Cut into squares.

These gooey brownies can be served as a dessert with scoops of vanilla ice-cream and warm chocolate sauce (see page 164).

1. Preheat the oven to 180°C/350°F/Gas Mark 4. Line a 18 x 28cm/7 x 11in roasting pan or can with baking parchment, snipping diagonally into the corners.

2. Dry-roast the hazelnuts and salt in a small frying pan over a low heat until the nuts are golden. Cool slightly, then chop very roughly.

3. Put the chocolate and butter in a large heatproof bowl and set over a saucepan of gently simmering water for 5 minutes, or until melted.

4. Whisk the eggs and sugar together until light and frothy, then gradually whisk in the melted chocolate mixture. Sift the flour and baking powder over the mixture and gently fold in. Fold in half the nuts, then pour the mixture into the prepared tin. Sprinkle with the remaining nuts and salt, and bake for 25–30 minutes, until well risen, the top is crusty and has begun to crack and the centre is still slightly soft. To test, insert a skewer into the centre: it should come out slightly sticky.

5. Sprinkle the fudge over the top, then put back in the oven for 2 minutes until it has just begun to soften. Leave the brownies to cool in the pan. When cool, lift out and peel away the paper.

6. To serve now, cut the brownie into small squares.

ALSO TRY
Replace the nuts and salt with 85g/3oz/⅔ cup dried sweetened cherries. In step 5, sprinkle with 85g/3oz roughly chopped mixed white chocolate and milk chocolate instead of fudge.

CHOCOLATE FONDANTS

A great freezer standby, smart enough to serve to friends and speedy enough to pop in the oven when you crave something indulgently chocolatey after a difficult day at work.

SERVES 8

PREP: 30 MINUTES, PLUS 1 HOUR CHILLING

COOK: 12–15 MINUTES

COOK FROM FROZEN: 20–25 MINUTES

140g/5oz/GENEROUS ½ CUP BUTTER, CUBED
4 TSP UNSWEETENED COCOA POWDER
140g/5oz DARK CHOCOLATE, BROKEN INTO PIECES
2 EGGS AND 2 EGG YOLKS
115g/4oz/GENEROUS ½ CUP CASTER (SUPERFINE) SUGAR
25g/1oz/3 TBSP PLAIN (ALL-PURPOSE) FLOUR
ICING (CONFECTIONERS') SUGAR, TO SERVE

Coffee sauce

85g/3oz/6 TBSP BUTTER
85g/3oz/SCANT ½ CUP LIGHT BROWN SUGAR
250ml/ 8fl oz/1 CUP DOUBLE (HEAVY) CREAM
2 TSP INSTANT COFFEE

1. Melt 25g/1oz/2 tbsp of the butter and brush the insides of 8 x 200ml/7fl oz/⅞ cup metal dessert moulds. Add ½ tsp cocoa to each, then tilt and tap the moulds to coat them evenly with cocoa and tap out the excess.

2. Put the remaining butter and the dark chocolate in a large bowl and set this over a saucepan of gently simmering water for 5 minutes, until melted. Stir gently, then remove the bowl and set aside.

3. Whisk the eggs, egg yolks and sugar together in a large heatproof bowl using an electric whisk for about 5 minutes, until very thick. Lift the whisk a little; as the mixture falls from it, it should leave a ribbon-like trail that stays on the surface for a few seconds. If you have a handheld electric mixer, you can speed up the process by setting the bowl over the pan of simmering water.

Recipe continues...

To serve from frozen

Preheat the oven to 180°C/350°F/Gas Mark 4. Cook the fondants from frozen for 20-25 minutes, until well risen, the tops are crusty and the centres still slightly soft. For each fondant, pop out some of the sauce ice-cubes into a bowl, microwave on full power for 20 seconds, then stir until smooth and hot. Dust the desserts with sifted icing sugar and serve with scoops of ice-cream and a drizzle of the coffee sauce.

4. Pour the melted butter-and-chocolate mixture into the whisked eggs and gently fold together. Sift the flour over the surface and gently fold in. Divide the mixture among the cocoa-lined moulds. Leave to cool completely.

5. To make the sauce, heat the butter and sugar in a small saucepan until the sugar has dissolved, then boil for 1 minute. Take off the heat, add the cream and coffee and stir until the coffee has dissolved; leave to cool.

6. To serve, chill the desserts for 1 hour. Preheat the oven to 180°C/350°F/Gas Mark 4. Cook the desserts for 12–15 minutes, until well risen, the tops are crusty and the centres still slightly soft. Reheat the sauce. Serve the puddings in the moulds or loosen the edges with a knife and turn out, dust with sifted icing sugar and serve with scoops of ice-cream and a drizzle of the sauce.

To freeze

At the end of step 4, cover each pudding mould with foil. Label, then freeze for up to 2 months. At the end of step 5, pour the sauce into an ice-cube tray and freeze until firm. Pop out the cubes into a plastic bag, seal, label and return to the freezer.

COOK'S TIPS

These puddings can be cooked in disposable foil pudding cups: it saves on washing-up and means that your metal moulds aren't out of action for weeks.

Instead of the coffee sauce, you might like to serve this dessert with melba sauce (see page 166) and a few halved strawberries, or apricot and orange sauce (see page 167).

Don't throw away the 2 egg whites after using the yolks: freeze and use when making meringue. Pack in a small plastic container, label and freeze for up to 2 months. Thaw at room temperature for 2–3 hours, or overnight in the fridge.

MAPLE PECAN PIE

SERVES 8
PREP: 50 MINUTES, PLUS 20 MINUTES CHILLING
COOK: 45–50 MINUTES
REHEAT FROM FROZEN: 45 MINUTES

Pastry

175g/6oz/1½ CUPS PLAIN (ALL-PURPOSE) FLOUR,
   PLUS EXTRA FOR DUSTING
1 TSP GROUND CINNAMON
85g/3oz/6 TBSP BUTTER, COLD AND CUBED
55g/2oz/4 TBSP CASTER (SUPERFINE) SUGAR
2 EGG YOLKS

Maple pecan filling

175ml/6fl oz/GENEROUS ½ CUP MAPLE SYRUP
175g/6oz/GENEROUS ¾ CUP LIGHT BROWN SUGAR
85g/3oz/6 TBSP BUTTER
3 EGGS
½ TSP GROUND CINNAMON
1 TSP VANILLA EXTRACT
140g/5oz/1½ CUPS PECAN NUTS

This tart can be reheated from frozen and is fabulous served warm with softly whipped cream flavoured with a little ground cinnamon or a splash of Bourbon or Scotch whisky and a teaspoonful of brown sugar.

1. To make the pastry, sift the flour and cinnamon into a bowl, add the butter and rub in until it resembles fine crumbs. Stir in the sugar, then the egg yolks, and bring together to make a ball, adding 1–2 tsp cold water if necessary. Knead very lightly on a lightly floured surface, then roll out thinly until a little larger than a 24cm/9½in loose-bottomed fluted tart tin.

2. Lift the pastry over a rolling pin and unroll into the tart tin; press into the fluted edge. Trim the pastry a little above the rim of the tin to allow for shrinkage. Prick the bottom with a fork, then chill for 20 minutes.

3. Preheat the oven to 190°C/375°F/Gas Mark 5. Place the tart tin on a baking sheet and line the pastry with baking parchment and dried beans. Bake for 10 minutes. Remove the paper and beans and cook for another 5 minutes, until the pastry is dry and the top edges just beginning to colour. Set aside. Reduce the oven to 180°C/350°F/Gas Mark 4.

Recipe continues

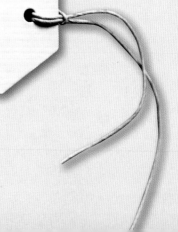

To freeze
After step 5, leave to cool completely. Freeze in the tin until firm. Take out of the tin, wrap in foil and label. Freeze for up to 2 months.

4. Meanwhile, make the filling. Put the maple syrup, brown sugar and butter in a saucepan and heat gently, stirring from time to time, until the sugar has dissolved. Leave to cool while the pastry cooks.

5. Beat the eggs, cinnamon and vanilla together, then gradually beat into the cooled syrup mixture. Pour into the cooked pastry case and scatter the pecan nuts over the top. Bake for about 30–35 minutes, or until slightly risen and the centre softly set. Check after 20 minutes or so and cover the top loosely with foil if the nuts seem to be browning too quickly. Leave to cool for 30 minutes.

6. Serve while still warm, with whipped cream.

To serve from frozen

Preheat the oven to 160°C/325°F/Gas Mark 3. Unwrap the pie, put it back in the tin and place on a baking sheet. Loosely cover with foil and reheat from frozen for 45 minutes.

COOK'S TIPS
- Stir 55g/2oz roughly chopped dark chocolate into the warmed maple syrup mixture as you take the pan off the heat so that it melts in the residual heat; then add the eggs as above.
- If the cooked pastry case appears to have a crack, after baking blind, brush the inside with beaten egg to 'glue' the crack together and put it back in the oven for a few minutes to set the egg before adding the filling.

ICES

ICES

While ice-cream might seem the most obvious thing to have in your deep freeze, not many of us get round to making our own. A scoop of homemade ice-cream is the perfect accompaniment to many desserts, and you don't need any special skill or equipment to make it. The secret is to beat the ice-cream as it freezes so that the ice crystals remain small, resulting in a creamy texture. This can be done with a fork or a handheld blender, or by transferring the ice-cream to a food processor and beating it for a minute or two before returning it to the freezer.

The time it takes to freeze the ice-cream will vary depending on the container. If you are in a hurry, a large loaf tin or small roasting pan works well as the metal chills down fast and speeds up the freezing. A plastic container saves on washing-up, as the ice-cream can be beaten and stored in the same container, but will add an hour or two to the chilling. The thinner the layer of ice-cream, the faster it will freeze. If you are an ice-cream enthusiast, you might want an electric ice-cream machine: it will churn and freeze a batch of ice-cream in around 30 minutes.

Vanilla ice-cream is popular and versatile. You can serve it with fruit or chocolate sauce (see page 166), marble it with a thick raspberry sauce and refreeze for a nostalgic raspberry ripple (see page 164), or fold in rum-soaked raisins and wrap in a flourless sponge to make a special roulade (see page 162). A refreshing berry sorbet can be made with mixed berries or a single variety of fruit (see page 168). And for kids and the young at heart, ice lollipops (see page 170) can be smooth and fruity or have an alcoholic kick; for fun, dip them in melted chocolate and sugar sprinkles.

CHOCOLATE ROULADE
WITH RUM AND RAISIN ICE-CREAM

SERVES 6

PREP: 45 MINUTES, PLUS COOLING

COOK: 15 MINUTES

FREEZE: OVERNIGHT

SERVE FROM FROZEN

125ml/4fl oz/½ CUP DARK RUM

2 TBSP RUNNY HONEY

115g/4oz/SCANT ¾ CUP RAISINS

1 LITRE/1¾ PINT/4 CUPS SOFT-SCOOP VANILLA ICE-CREAM
    HOT CHOCOLATE SAUCE, TO SERVE (SEE PAGE 166)

Chocolate sponge

200g/7oz DARK CHOCOLATE, BROKEN INTO PIECES

5 EGGS, SEPARATED

175g/6oz/GENEROUS ¾ CUP CASTER (SUPERFINE)
    SUGAR, PLUS EXTRA FOR SPRINKLING

To freeze
At the end of step 7, freeze for up to 2 months.

To serve from frozen
Unwrap, cut into thick slices using a hot knife and transfer to plates.

If you are of a certain generation, you may remember the Arctic roll, a log-shaped sponge with an ice-cream centre. This is a sophisticated version, made with a flourless chocolate sponge around vanilla ice-cream spiked with rum-soaked raisins.

1. Pour the rum into a small saucepan, bring almost to the boil, then stir in the honey and raisins. Cover, simmer for 3 minutes, then set aside to soak for at least 4 hours, or overnight.

2. To make the roulade, preheat the oven to 180°C/350°F/ Gas Mark 4. Line a 35 x 23cm/13 x 9in deep roasting pan with baking parchment, snipping diagonally into the corners.

3. Melt the chocolate in a heatproof bowl set over a saucepan of gently simmering water. Whisk the egg whites in a large bowl until stiff. Gradually whisk in one-third of the sugar, a teaspoonful at a time, until thick. In a separate bowl, whisk the yolks with the remaining sugar until pale and thick; the whisk should leave a trail when lifted.

4. Fold the melted chocolate into the egg yolk mixture, then fold in a large spoonful of the whites to loosen the mixture. Add the remaining egg whites and fold in gently until there are no specks of egg white.

5. Pour the mixture into the prepared tin, tilting it to ease the mixture into the corners and to make an even layer. Bake for 15 minutes, or until the top is crusty and the sponge just set. Leave to cool in the tin for several hours.

6. Fold the rum-soaked raisins into the ice-cream and freeze for ½–1 hour, until thick enough to scoop.

7. Place a piece of baking parchment on a work surface and sprinkle lightly with caster sugar. Turn the chocolate sponge out on to the parchment so a short side is nearest you. Peel away the parchment, then spoon the ice-cream evenly over the top. Roll up the sponge, starting with the short edge nearest you; it will crack as you roll it, but don't worry. Quickly wrap the paper around to make a good rounded shape. Overwrap the paper with foil, twist the ends to seal, then freeze for 4 hours, or ideally overnight.

8. Serve slices of the roulade with the hot chocolate sauce.

RASPBERRY RIPPLE ICE CREAM

SERVES 4

PREP: 25 MINUTES, PLUS 30 MINUTES COOLING

COOK: 10 MINUTES

FREEZE: OVERNIGHT

SERVE FROM FROZEN: 10 MINUTES AT
ROOM TEMPERATURE

Vanilla ice-cream

1 VANILLA POD, SLIT LENGTHWAYS
300ml/10fl oz/1¼ CUPS FULL-FAT (WHOLE) MILK
85g/3oz/SCANT ½ CUP CASTER (SUPERFINE) SUGAR
4 EGG YOLKS
1 TSP CORNFLOUR (CORNSTARCH)
300ml/10fl oz/1¼ CUPS DOUBLE (HEAVY) CREAM

Raspberry ripple

450g/1lb/3½ CUPS RASPBERRIES
225g/8oz/GENEROUS 1 CUP PRESERVING SUGAR
WITH PECTIN
15g/½oz/1 TBSP BUTTER

To freeze
Freeze for up to 2 months.

To serve from frozen
Leave to soften for
10 minutes at room
temperature, or until soft
enough to scoop.

A deluxe version of a childhood favourite. The vanilla ice-cream can be served on its own or drizzled with one of the sauces on pages 166-167 for a luscious ice-cream sundae. Vanilla pods are expensive: vanilla bean paste is a good alternative. Sold in small jars, it is a sugar suspension with lots of tiny black vanilla seeds. If using the paste, add it to the thickened milk, sugar and egg yolk mixture in step 2.

1. If you have an electric ice-cream machine, chill it according to the manufacturer's instructions.

2. Scrape the vanilla seeds from the pod, using a small knife, then place both pod and seeds in a saucepan with the milk. Bring slowly to the boil, then take off the heat and leave to stand for 30 minutes for the flavour to develop. Lift out the pod (you can rinse it with warm water and dry it, then use it to flavour a jar of sugar).

3. Mix the sugar, egg yolks and cornflour together until smooth. Reheat the milk and gradually whisk into the sugar mixture. Pour back into the pan and slowly bring just to the boil over a low heat, stirring constantly, until thickened and smooth. Cover the surface with crumpled and wetted baking parchment and leave to cool.

4. Meanwhile, make the raspberry ripple. Put the raspberries in a large saucepan, sprinkle over the sugar, then crush the berries with a vegetable masher. Add the butter and heat gently until the sugar has dissolved. Increase the heat and boil rapidly for 2–5 minutes, until the mixture falls slowly and thickly from a wooden spoon. Cool for a few minutes, then press through a sieve into a bowl and discard the seeds. Leave to cool completely.

5. Mix the cream (no need to whip first) into the cooled custard, then pour into the cooled ice-cream machine. Churn for 20–30 minutes, until thick. Without an ice-cream machine, lightly whip the cream until soft peaks form. Fold it into the custard, then pour into a 900g/2lb non-stick loaf tin. Freeze for 4–6 hours, until thick, beating once or twice with a fork to break up the ice crystals.

6. Add alternate spoonfuls of ice-cream and raspberry purée to a clean loaf tin or plastic container, then marble together by running a knife through the mixture.

7. Cover the container with clingfilm (plastic wrap) or a lid, seal and label. Freeze overnight.

Ice-cream flavours

- Strawberry ripple – replace the raspberries with the same weight of strawberries.
- Cookies and cream – make up vanilla ice-cream and fold in 140g/5oz roughly crumbled chunky chocolate and nut cookies after churning.
- Dark chocolate – stir 200g/7oz dark chocolate, broken into pieces, into the hot custard in step 2, until just melted. Cool, then continue as in step 4.
- Double chocolate – stir 140g/5oz white chocolate, broken into pieces, into the hot custard in step 2, until just melted. Cool, then continue as in step 4. When the ice-cream is almost set, stir in another 100g/3½oz diced milk chocolate, or half milk and half white chocolate.
- Pistachio – add 115g/4oz/ scant 1 cup finely chopped pistachios and a few drops of green food colouring when adding the cream in step 4.
- Orange and ginger – add the finely grated zest of 1 orange and 85g/3oz finely chopped preserved ginger with the cream in step 4.

EASY ICE-CREAM SAUCES

Liven up a scoop of ice-cream with a drizzle of homemade sauce. For a treat, layer ice-cream and sauce in glasses, adding fruit, crushed meringues, choc chip cookies or chocolate brownies, and finish with sweets, mini marshmallows or a sprinkling of popping candy.

ALL RECIPES SERVE 6

CHOCOLATE SAUCE

PREP: 5 MINUTES

COOK: 5 MINUTES

Break 140g/5oz dark chocolate into pieces and place in a saucepan with 15g/½oz/1 tbsp butter, 3 tbsp caster (superfine) sugar, 150ml/5fl oz/⅔ cup milk and a pinch of ground cinnamon. Heat very gently, stirring from time to time, until the sauce is smooth and glossy. Serve warm or cold. You might like to add a little finely chopped red chilli or 1–2 tbsp brandy or rum.

To freeze
Leave any of the sauces to cool, then pour into sections of an ice-cube tray. Freeze until hard, then either leave in the tray, wrap in clingfilm (plastic wrap) and label, or pop out the cubes into a plastic bag, seal and label. Freeze for up to 2 months.

MELBA SAUCE

PREP: 5 MINUTES

Put 225g/8oz/1¾ cups raspberries in a blender or food processor, add the juice of ½ lemon and 2 tbsp icing (confectioners') sugar and purée until smooth. Press through a sieve to discard the seeds. Serve cold. Strawberry or mixed summer berry sauce can be made in the same way.

BLUEBERRY SAUCE

PREP: 2 MINUTES

COOK: 5 MINUTES

Put 4 tsp cornflour (cornstarch) and 4 tbsp caster (superfine) sugar in a saucepan, gradually mix in 175ml/6fl oz/¾ cup water, then add 250g/9oz/generous 1½ cups blueberries. Bring to the boil over a low heat, then simmer for 3–4 minutes, stirring, until the blueberries are just softened and the sauce is a deep colour. Serve warm or cold.

TOFFEE SAUCE

PREP: 2 MINUTES

COOK: 3–4 MINUTES

Melt 85g/3oz/6 tbsp butter in a saucepan with 85g/3oz/scant ½ cup soft brown sugar, mix in a 400g can full-fat (whole) condensed milk and cook over a medium-low heat, stirring continuously, for 3–4 minutes, until the sauce smells of toffee. Be careful not to have the heat too high, or the milk may catch on the bottom of the pan. Serve warm or cold.

APRICOT
AND ORANGE SAUCE

PREP: 5 MINUTES

COOK: 10 MINUTES

Put 200g/7oz/1 generous cup ready-to-eat dried (plumped) apricots in a saucepan with 250ml/ 8fl oz/1 cup water, bring to the boil, then cover and simmer gently for 10 minutes. Purée the apricots and water in a blender or food processor with 2 tbsp caster (superfine) sugar and the juice of 2 oranges. Add a little extra water if needed to make a pouring consistency. For a scented Middle Eastern flavour, add 4 roughly crushed cardamom pods and their black seeds to the pan with the apricots – pick out the pods before puréeing.

MANGO
AND LIME SAUCE

PREP: 5 MINUTES

COOK: 5 MINUTES

Dice the flesh from 2 large mangoes and place in a saucepan with 4 tbsp water, 4 tbsp caster (superfine) sugar and the grated zest and juice of 2 limes. Cover and simmer gently for 5 minutes, then purée in a blender or food processor until smooth. Serve warm or cold.

SPICED BLACKBERRY
AND RED WINE SAUCE

PREP: 2 MINUTES

COOK: 5 MINUTES

Put 125ml/4fl oz/½ cup red wine, 125ml/ 4fl oz/½ cup water, 4 tbsp caster (superfine) sugar, 3 cloves and a 5cm/2in piece of cinnamon stick in a saucepan and heat gently, stirring, until the sugar has dissolved. Add 225g/8oz/1½ cups blackberries, and 1 tbsp cornflour (cornstarch) mixed with 2 tbsp cold water, and cook over a medium heat for 4–5 minutes, stirring, until the blackberries are softened and the sauce thickened. Discard the spices and serve the sauce warm or cold.

To serve from frozen

For a single serving of any of these sauces, microwave 2 or 3 sauce cubes in a small bowl in 10-second bursts on full power until soft enough to stir, then continue until piping hot. Or microwave the full quantity in 30-second bursts, stirring once or twice until smooth and hot. To reheat in a small saucepan, cover and heat very gently for 5-10 minutes, stirring from time to time, until smooth and hot.

RUBY RED BERRY SORBET

Capture the essence of summer in this easy berry sorbet. You could use just a single variety of berry, or try other fruit such as mango. Keep the total prepared weight of fruit the same and omit the mint if you like. Serve with extra berries, or drizzle with blueberry sauce (see page 166).

SERVES 4–6

PREP: 20 MINUTES, PLUS 30 MINUTES INFUSING

COOK: 8 MINUTES

FREEZE: 25–30 MINUTES IN AN ICE-CREAM MACHINE,
OR 6 HOURS IN THE FREEZER

SERVE FROM FROZEN: 10 MINUTES AT ROOM TEMPERATURE

LEAVES FROM 3 SPRIGS OF FRESH MINT

140g/5oz/¾ CUP CASTER (SUPERFINE) SUGAR

500g/1lb 2oz/4 CUPS MIXED FRESH SUMMER BERRIES,
SUCH AS STRAWBERRIES, RASPBERRIES
AND LOGANBERRIES, HULLED

JUICE OF ½ LEMON

1 EGG WHITE

1. If you have an electric ice-cream machine, chill it according to the manufacturer's instructions.

2. Put the mint, sugar and 250ml/8fl oz/1 cup water in a saucepan and heat gently, stirring from time to time, until the sugar dissolves. Bring to the boil, then boil for 3 minutes, until syrupy. Take off the heat and set aside for 30 minutes for the flavour to develop.

3. Purée the berries in a blender or food processor, then press through a sieve into a bowl and discard the seeds. Mix the purée with the lemon juice, then stir in the cooled strained sugar syrup.

4. Pour into the cooled electric ice-cream machine and churn for 15 minutes, until the sorbet is just beginning to thicken. Lightly whisk the egg white until frothy, then beat into the sorbet and churn for another 10–15 minutes, or until very thick.

5. If you don't have an ice-cream machine, pour the mixture into a 900g/2lb loaf tin and freeze for 4 hours; beat with a fork to break up the ice crystals when semi-frozen. Lightly whisk the egg white until frothy, then beat into the sorbet and freeze for 2 hours, or until firm enough to scoop.

To freeze
Freeze for up to 2 months.

To serve
If the sorbet has been in the freezer overnight or longer, leave to soften for 10 minutes at room temperatue, until soft enough to scoop into dishes or cones.

COCONUT AND LIME SORBET

Put 140g/5oz/¾ cup caster (superfine) sugar and 250ml/8fl oz/1 cup water in a saucepan and heat gently, stirring from time to time, until the sugar has dissolved, then boil for 3 minutes. Pour in 400ml can full-fat (whole) coconut milk, add the grated zest and juice of 1 lime and whisk until smooth. Leave to cool, then chill in the fridge. Pour into a cooled electric ice-cream machine and churn for 20–30 minutes, until firm enough to scoop. Alternatively pour into a 900g/2lb non-stick loaf tin and freeze for 4–6 hours, beating once or twice with a fork to break up the ice crystals. Transfer to a plastic container, freeze and serve as above.

ICE POPS

Fill up the odd space in the freezer with a few ice pops. Ice-pop moulds can be bought in cookshops, department stores and most large supermarkets. To serve, dip the mould into a bowl filled with hot water from the tap, count to three, then flex each mould slightly and ease the ice pop from it.

ALL RECIPES SERVE 6

ICED COFFEE LIQUEUR

Mix 250ml/8fl oz/1 cup strong fresh coffee (2 heaped tbsp ground coffee with 300ml/10fl oz/1¼ cups boiling water in a cafetière, stand 5 minutes, then strain) with 2 tbsp soft brown sugar, 4 tbsp double (heavy) cream and 4 tbsp coffee cream liqueur. Cool, then pour into ice-pop moulds. Freeze until firm.

LEMON AND LIME CRUSH

Pare the rind from 4 unwaxed lemons using a vegetable peeler, taking care to peel off as little white pith as possible, as this would make the ice pops bitter. Put the pared rind in a saucepan with 450ml/16fl oz/2 cups water and 140g/5oz/ ¾ cup caster (superfine) sugar, heat gently until the sugar has dissolved, then boil for 5 minutes. Leave to cool. Strain into a jug, add the juice from 2 limes, then pour into ice-pop moulds, adding a sprig of mint to each one if liked. Freeze until firm.

BANANA CUSTARD

Mash or purée 350g/12oz (2 large) bananas with the juice of ½ lemon, then mix with 225g/8oz/1 cup canned custard. Pour into ice-pop moulds and freeze until firm.

Dip the moulds into hot water and remove the ice pops, then dip the tip of each ice pop in 85g/3oz melted milk chocolate and sprinkle over multi-coloured sugar sprinkles. Put back into the freezer on a baking sheet lined with baking parchment until firm. Wrap individually in clingfilm (plastic wrap) and pack in a plastic container before refreezing until firm.

WATERMELON AND LIME

Put 3 tbsp caster (superfine) sugar and 3 tbsp water in a saucepan and heat gently, stirring from time to time, until the sugar has dissolved. Bring to the boil and cook for 1 minute. Take off the heat and add the grated zest and juice of 1 lime. Purée 350g/12oz deseeded and diced watermelon in a blender or food processor, stir into the syrup and leave to cool. Pour into ice-pop moulds and freeze until firm.

PEACH BELLINIS

Halve, stone and slice 350g/12oz (about 4) ripe peaches. Place in a saucepan with 2 tbsp caster (superfine) sugar and 2 tbsp water, cover and simmer gently for 10 minutes, or until the peaches are soft. Purée in a blender or food processor until smooth, then rub through a sieve to discard the skins. Stir in 250ml/8fl oz/1 cup Prosecco or other dry sparkling white wine. Pour into ice-pop moulds and freeze until firm.

STRAWBERRY YOGURT

Purée 250g/9oz strawberries, then rub through a sieve, discarding the seeds. Mix with 115g/4oz/½ cup Greek-style Yogurt with Coconut, or plain Greek Yogurt and 1 tbsp runny honey. Pour into ice-pop moulds and freeze until firm.

STOCK

It takes just minutes to get a pot of stock on the go. Our mothers and grandmothers knew a thing or two about recycling, but to them it was simply good practice or the sign of a thrifty cook to use the trimmings from the top of leeks or celery, small and mis-shapen carrots, a cooked chicken carcass, or leftover bones, shells and flesh from filleting fish or peeling shellfish. Strain and then freeze in conveniently sized packs to make into soups, sauces or gravy or to use in casseroles and risottos.

To freeze

Pack into conveniently sized plastic bags, allowing some space because the stock will expand as it freezes. Seal tightly and label. Freeze for up to 3 months.

To serve from frozen

Take out of the bag and thaw in a bowl in the microwave, or in a covered saucepan, or overnight in the fridge (the time depends on the size of the bag). Add to your chosen recipe and reheat thoroughly.

FISH STOCK

MAKES ABOUT 1.5 LITRES/2¾ PINTS/1½ QUARTS
PREP: 10 MINUTES
COOK: 45 MINUTES

900g/2lb MIXED FISH TRIMMINGS, INCLUDING HEADS, BACKBONES, TAILS,
    SKINS AND PRAWN SHELLS
1 ONION, QUARTERED
TOPS FROM 2 LEEKS OR 1 EXTRA ONION, THICKLY SLICED
2 CELERY STICKS, SLICED
2 CARROTS, SLICED
HANDFUL OF FRESH PARSLEY OR TARRAGON STALKS
PARED RIND FROM 1 UNWAXED LEMON
½ TSP SALT
½ TSP WHITE PEPPERCORNS

1. Put all the ingredients in a saucepan, add 1.7 litres/3 pints/1¾ quarts cold water and bring slowly to the boil. Remove any greyish foam using a slotted spoon, then partially cover the pan and simmer gently for 30 minutes. Don't cook fish heads for longer than 30 minutes, or the stock will taste bitter.

2. Strain into a bowl, then return the stock to the pan and cook for another 15 minutes to concentrate the flavours.

BEEF STOCK

MAKES ABOUT 2.5 LITRES/4½ PINTS/2½ QUARTS

PREP: 10 MINUTES

COOK: ABOUT 4 HOURS

1.8kg/4lb MIXED BEEF BONES, SHIN, RIB OR SAWN MARROW BONES

2 TBSP SUNFLOWER OIL

4 SLICES STREAKY BACON, ROUGHLY CHOPPED

2 ONIONS, ROUGHLY CHOPPED

2 CARROTS, SLICED

3 CELERY STICKS, SLICED

2–3 SPRIGS OF THYME

2 BAY LEAVES

½ TSP SALT

½ TSP BLACK PEPPERCORNS

1. Preheat the oven to 190°C/375°F/Gas Mark 5. Put the bones in a roasting pan, drizzle with 1 tbsp oil and cook for 45 minutes, or until browned.

2. Heat the remaining oil in a large saucepan over a low heat, add the bacon and onions and cook gently for 10 minutes, until the onions are softened and deep golden.

3. Add the carrots, celery, herbs, salt, pepper and browned bones, and 2.8 litres/5 pints/scant 3 quarts cold water. If necessary, add a little more water so the bones are covered by about 5cm/2in of water. Bring the water slowly to the boil over a low heat. Remove any greyish foam using a slotted spoon, then partially cover the pan and simmer gently for 3 hours.

4. Strain the stock into a bowl. Taste and adjust the seasoning. Leave to cool, then skim off the fat.

CHICKEN STOCK

Sometimes known as light stock, this is a great way to use the remains of a roast chicken. It can also be made with a roast pheasant or a guinea fowl carcass, but they are smaller, so reduce the amount of water. Aim to cover the carcass with 5cm/2in of water.

MAKES ABOUT 1.7 LITRES/3 PINTS/1¾ QUARTS

PREP: 10 MINUTES

COOK: 2 HOURS

1 ONION, QUARTERED, WITH THE INNER BROWN SKIN LEFT ON

TOPS FROM 2 LEEKS OR 1 EXTRA ONION, THICKLY SLICED

LEAFY TOPS FROM 1 BUNCH OF CELERY, OR 2 CELERY STICKS, SLICED

2 CARROTS, SLICED

1 COOKED CHICKEN CARCASS

½ TSP SALT

½ TSP BLACK PEPPERCORNS

SMALL BUNCH OF FRESH HERBS OR 2 DRIED BAY LEAVES

1. Put all the vegetables in a large saucepan, add the chicken carcass, breaking it into two pieces if necessary to fit into the pan. Pour over 2.3 litres/4 pints/2¼ quarts cold water, then add the salt, pepper and herbs.

2. Bring the water slowly to the boil over a low heat. Remove any greyish foam using a slotted spoon, then partially cover the pan and simmer gently for 2 hours.

3. Strain the stock into a bowl. Taste and adjust the seasoning. Leave to cool, then skim off the fat.

4. Use whatever you need and store the rest in the fridge for up to 3 days.

HOMEMADE STOCKS
...CONTINUED

COOK'S TIPS

• Taste the stock after straining: if it tastes a little thin, return to the saucepan and simmer, uncovered, for another 30 minutes, to reduce and concentrate the flavours.

• Add a splash of white wine, cider or dry sherry, some green leafy tops from celeriac (celery root) or fennel, a tomato or two and/or a few garlic cloves. You could also add the giblets or the neck from a fresh duck, pheasant or turkey.

• Stock can also be made in the oven: great if you have an Aga or Rayburn-style cooker that is constantly on. Reduce the amount of water slightly, as there will be very little evaporation. Preheat the oven to 180°C/350°F/Gas Mark.

• Bring all the ingredients to the boil in a flameproof casserole, then cover and transfer to the oven for 2 hours.

• If you don't have time to make chicken stock with the carcass left over from your roast, you can freeze the carcass in a plastic bag and make it into stock at a later date.

VEGETABLE STOCK

MAKES ABOUT 1.5 LITRES/2¾ PINTS/1½ QUARTS
PREP: 10 MINUTES
COOK: 55 MINUTES

1 TBSP OLIVE OIL
1 ONION, ROUGHLY CHOPPED
TOPS FROM 2 LEEKS OR 1 EXTRA ONION, SLICED
3 CARROTS, SLICED
4 CELERY STICKS, SLICED
4 TOMATOES, ROUGHLY CHOPPED
140g/5oz BUTTON MUSHROOMS, SLICED
SMALL BUNCH OF MIXED FRESH HERBS
½ TSP SALT
½ TSP BLACK PEPPERCORNS

1. Heat the oil in a large saucepan, add the onion and cook gently for 5 minutes, stirring, until softened. Add the leeks, carrots, celery, tomatoes and mushrooms and cook for another 5 minutes.

2. Add the herbs, salt, pepper and 2.4 litres/ 4 pints cold water. Bring slowly to the boil, skim off any greyish foam using a slotted spoon, then partially cover the pan and simmer gently for 45 minutes.

3. Strain into a bowl.

INDEX